THE ESSENTIAL GUIDE TO USING Mindfulness WITH CHILDREN & YOUNG PEOPLE

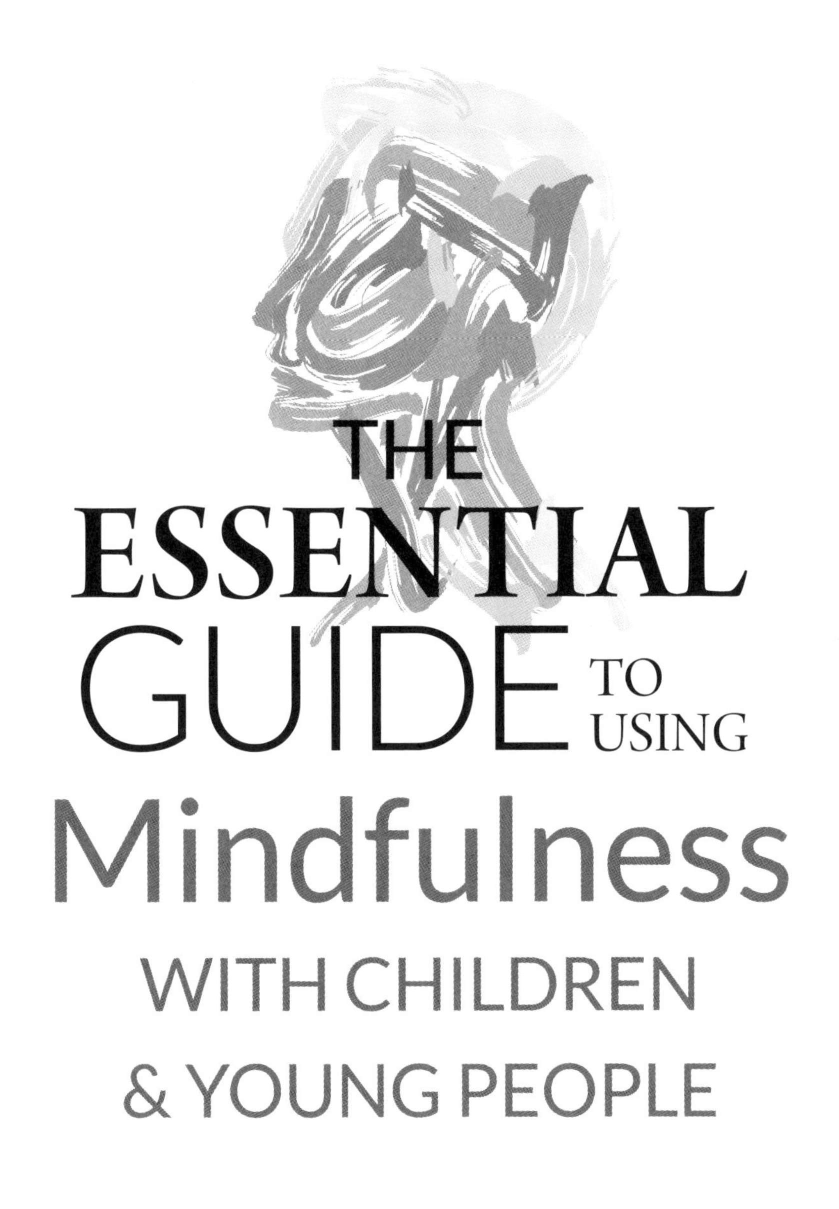

THE ESSENTIAL GUIDE TO USING Mindfulness WITH CHILDREN & YOUNG PEOPLE

TINA RAE, JODY WALSHE & JO WOOD

First published in 2017 by

Hinton House Publishers Ltd,
Newman House, 4 High Street, Buckingham, MK18 1NT, UK

T +44 (0)1280 822557 F +44 (0)1280 822338
E info@hintonpublishers.co.uk

www.hintonpublishers.com

British Library Cataloguing in Publication Data
A CIP catalogue record for this book is available from the British Library.

ISBN 978 1 906531 82 9

Printed and bound in the United Kingdom

The Hinton House Essential Guides

The Essential Guide to Using Mindfulness with Children & Young People

The Essential Guide to Using Solution-Focused Brief Therapy with Children & Young People

The Essential Guide to Using Cognitive Behavioural Therapy with Children & Young People

The Essential Guide to Using Positive Psychology with Children & Young People

The Hinton House Essential Guides are not intended to be used to deliver individual 'therapy' per se, but rather to contribute to the development of individual, small-group, or whole-class interventions, providing professionals with a series of tried-and-tested resources for use with young people. It is intended that they can be used not only to target those young people regarded as exhibiting behavioural problems, such as low self-esteem or anxiety, but that they may be used with all young people in order to prevent the escalation of any difficulties and to provide them with a range of therapeutic tools and problem-solving strategies and techniques to foster well-being and mental health.

The *Guides* are both educational and therapeutic in design, but are not, in any sense, a substitute for individualised interventions delivered by appropriate clinicians. However, the resources can and do provide useful tools for clinicians engaged in such individual interventions and school-based Learning Mentors/SENCOs/Inclusion Managers wishing to develop a programme of support for an individual student or groups of students in the school context and beyond.

These practical and user friendly guides are intended to provide a useful introduction to each approach or intervention, whilst also empowering professionals to safely make use of appropriate tools and strategies to foster emotional and psychological well-being.

Contents

Resources, Tables & Figures

About the Authors

Dr Tina Rae has more 30 years' experience working with children, adults and families in both clinical and educational contexts within local authorities and specialist educational services. She currently works as a Consultant Educational Psychologist in a range of SEMH and mainstream contexts and for *Compass Fostering* as a Consultant Psychologist, supporting foster carers, social workers and looked-after children. She was formerly an Academic and Professional Tutor for the Doctorate in Educational and Child Psychology at the University of East London (2010–2016). She is a registered member of the Health and Care Professions Council and a full member of the British Psychological Society. Tina is also a member of SEBDA (Social Emotional and Behavioural Difficulties Association), a member of ENSEC (European Network for Social and Emotional Competence) and a former trustee of the Nurture Group Network (NGN).

Tina has published more than 75 titles on topics including well-being, attachment, emotional literacy, behavioural problems, anger and stress management, critical incidents, cognitive behavioural therapy, motivational interviewing, solution-focused brief therapy, loss and bereavement in young people, youth offending and social skills development. Among her most recent publications are *Bouncing Back & Coping with Change* (2016), *Building Positive Thinking Habits* (2016) and *Understanding & Preventing Self-Harm in Schools* (2017), all from Hinton House Publishers.

Her current research is into staff well-being and resilience, including peer group supervision systems.

Tina is a regular speaker at both national and international conferences and events, and also provides training courses and supervision for school-based staff in both special and mainstream contexts and educational psychology services across the UK and internationally.

tinarae@hotmail.co.uk

Jody Walshe is an Educational Psychologist working in an outer London borough. Jody completed her doctorate in Educational and Child Psychology at the University of East London. Before commencing her training in educational psychology, Jody worked as a teacher, learning support assistant and tutor with young people aged between 5 and 19 years. The focus of much of her work was on addressing anxiety and mental health issues in school settings.

Jody's doctoral research explored the experiences, perceptions and training needs of secondary school staff working with self-harm.

Jody is the co-author of *Understanding and Preventing Self-Harm in Schools: Effective Strategies for Identifying Risk & Providing Support* (Hinton House, 2017) with Tina Rae.

Jo Wood is an Educational Psychologist working in an outer London Local Education Authority. Her doctoral research was on the use of Solution Circles to structure supervision for school staff.

Before beginning her training as an Educational Psychologist, Jo was a secondary school Science teacher in London for many years. She was also a Head of Science, teacher training fieldwork tutor, teaching assistant and tutor. Jo's last teaching job was three years as Head of Science in a Pupil Referral Unit in an inner London Borough.

An Introduction to Mindfulness

The key aim of this *Essential Guide* is to introduce the practice of mindfulness, which is an approach that can increase the life skills of children and young people by supporting them in developing the ability to both soothe and calm themselves, to pay attention to themselves in the world, and to think about and reflect upon both their actions and their relationships. At the outset it is important to point out that mindfulness is not simply an abstract body of knowledge. It is, in essence, a practical set of skills. For human beings daily living can often be extremely stressful and busy. The practice of mindfulness can support us in becoming more fully aware of living right now, in the present moment. There is an increasing body of research which shows that mindfulness can ultimately have long-term benefits for both our health and our levels of happiness.

Most of us, at some point, will have made a journey (for example, into work), and then on arrival suddenly realised that we don't actually remember engaging in the task of driving. There are also times when we may be lying in a bath or having a shower and feeling the warm water on our bodies, but not actually being present in that moment. Very often we will be thinking about something that we have to do or an event that has previously taken place, or a meeting that we might need to organise. Many of us can become entrenched in living our lives almost as if on automatic pilot. We barely live in the present and don't pay attention to what is happening in our lives in a particular moment. However, if we stop to really think about the situation that moment is actually all that we have.

Mindfulness is paying attention here and now with kindness and curiosity.

Association for Mindfulness in Education (from website)

Mindfulness has also been described as:

the awareness that emerges through paying attention on purpose through the present moment, non-judgementally, to the unfolding of experience moment by moment.

Kabat-Zinn et al 2007

One of the simplest ways to get into a mindful state is to sit down on a chair, close your eyes and begin to focus on your breathing. As you sit still, relaxed but also alert, you can then direct your attention to the sensation of each inhalation and exhalation, and also become aware of the feeling of air as it enters and then leaves your mouth or nostrils. It is whilst doing this that other thoughts will enter into your mind. The idea is to become aware of such intrusions, noting each of these in turn without judgement, and then simply let them pass. This is one of the key elements of mindfulness and the skill that is focused upon throughout the '60 Mindful Minutes' programme for young children.

The Benefits of Mindfulness

During the last 20 to 25 years numerous studies have demonstrated that mindfulness can provide benefits in a range of clinical settings, from pain management to stress relief, through to management of depression. Work has also been highlighted in non-clinical groups (Baer, 2003; Greeson, 2009). Mindfulness training has at least five broad beneficial effects. It promotes:

- Increased sensory awareness
- Greater cognitive control
- Enhanced regulation of emotions
- Acceptance of transient thoughts and feelings
- The capacity to regulate attention

Sensory awareness

Practising mindfulness nurtures the capacity to bring our sensory experience into our consciousness. This enables us to create the space to simply stop and just 'be', experiencing the moment in all its fullness. Being able to be in the moment and appreciate the positive sensory experiences that we have is not simply enjoyable, it also elicits positive emotions that feed into overall well-being, according to Barbara Frederickson of the University of North Carolina (2009). In her research she has demonstrated that recurrently experiencing positive emotions simultaneously broadens our sensory awareness, thus creating further opportunities for sensory savouring. This also increases overall psychological and emotional resilience.

Cognitive control

The goal of mindfulness is not to simply eliminate from the mind all thoughts and feelings, but also to anchor oneself to what one is currently experiencing in the sensory world. The idea is to allow thoughts to enter the mind quite freely and to simply note these in a non-judgemental and unanalytical manner. This is particularly useful in terms of managing busy minds: in effect, mindfulness promotes a de-centred perspective on the copious thoughts that we all have. It enables us to create a distance between the thoughts that we have and our cognitive reactions to them. We can have a thought without actually having to act upon it. We can treat it simply as a thought.

Emotional regulation

It is very easy to become overwhelmed by intrusive emotional thoughts. These often reflect uncomfortable situations that have caused us to feel angry, embarrassed or stressed. Mindfulness encourages a more de-centred perspective on such feelings. Once again the feelings should be noted and allowed to pass. If we choose just to recognise the feelings, then we provide ourselves with the opportunity to decide how to respond to them, rather than reacting automatically and engaging in patterns of automatic negative thinking, which always tend to lead to less positive outcomes for the individual.

Acceptance of transient thoughts and feelings

Treating our thoughts in this non-judgemental and more detached manner is also hugely positive in terms of accepting our thoughts and feelings. This is very important, as it encourages us to be more tolerant and kind to ourselves. We do not need to beat ourselves up for having negative or intrusive thoughts or feelings; we simply have to accept them and know that we need to learn to be kinder to ourselves in both the short and longer term.

Attention regulation

As mindfulness does not demand that we clear our minds of all thoughts and feelings, but rather that we allow them to pass by and be noted, this, in effect, provides us with training in how to regulate and direct our attention at will. This is extremely important for young children in learning contexts. Being able to bring back wandering attention over and over again is, according to William James, 'the very route of judgement, character and will' (1980). In his *The Principles of Psychology*, James highlights that education should improve this faculty and, if it does, it is then 'the education par excellence'.

Positive psychology

Mindfulness is a branch of positive psychology, which is 'the scientific study of optimal human functioning and what makes life worth living' (Grenville-Cleave, 2012, p.1). Positive psychology was recognised as a formal branch of psychology from 1998, and was proposed first by Martin Seligman and Mihaly Csíkszentmihályi (Grenville-Cleave, 2012). It offers a shift in thought away from traditional psychology's focus on the reduction of distress and disorder to a strengths-based approach, which builds and fosters the individual's strengths and resilience (Ciarrochi et al., 2013). Positive psychologists believe that there is more to life than the absence of distress and disorder and this branch of psychology encourages the study of how people thrive. It considers the development of positive individual traits, such as the capacity for love, courage, interpersonal competence, perseverance and forgiveness, amongst others (Ciarrochi et al., 2013). Davis (2012) suggests that mindfulness encourages some of the subjective states of well-being referred to by positive psychologists, such as calmness, vitality, spaciousness and freedom (Csíkszentmihályi, 1991; Seligman, 2002).

Mindfulness Research with Adults

Mindfulness has become more and more popular in recent years and there is a growing body of evidence for its efficacy. Mindfulness-based stress reduction (MBSR) was pioneered by Jon

Kabat-Zinn and was established as an intervention to help those with chronic physical illnesses and attendant emotional stress. Mindfulness-based cognitive therapy (MBCT) (Williams & Penman, 2011) focuses on addressing depression and is recommended as a treatment for depression by the National Institute of Clinical Excellence (NICE) in its guidelines, *Depression: the Treatment and Management of Depression in Adults* (2009).

There is an ever-growing body of evidence that looks at the impact of mindfulness on adults with mental health issues such as depression, anxiety and stress. Hofmann et al.'s (2010) meta-review identified robust effective sizes to support moderate efficacy of mindfulness-based therapy for improving anxiety. Rasmussen and Pidgeon (2011) found that mindfulness was a significant predictor of low levels of social anxiety and high levels of self-esteem; assessed through self-reporting.

Virgili's (2013) meta-analysis explored the impact of mindfulness for working adults on reducing stress, depression and anxiety. The review of 19 mindfulness-based interventions, with a total of 1,139 participants, found medium to large effects resulting from mindfulness meditation, and that this was mostly sustained when reviewed around five weeks later.

Neuropsychology has also provided empirical support for the effects of mindfulness. Davidson et al. (2003) found significant increases in left-sided anterior activation, a pattern associated with positive affect, demonstrating that mindfulness meditation produces discernible effects on brain function. Davidson's (2008) brain imaging research found that mindfulness meditation alters the functions and structure of the brain, resulting in improved quality of emotion and thought. Weare (2012, p.4) notes that brain imaging studies with adults show mindfulness meditation to reliably and significantly 'alter the structure and function of the brain to improve the quality of both thought and feeling'. These neuropsychological pieces of research provide further, robust, evidence for the impact of mindfulness. However, it is important to note that there remains debate about neuropsychology's assumption that isolated brain regions are responsible for specific psychological functions (Eysenck & Keane, 2010).

Mindfulness Research with Children, Young People and in Schools

The benefits of mindfulness for children and young people is not evidenced in as much detail, although the body of research is growing quickly and current findings suggest it can be very positive.

Historically, it has generally been the case that mindfulness has been used in a clinical context by practitioners who are aiming to support those suffering with stress, anxiety and depression. However, it has become increasingly apparent that using mindfulness as a preventative tool for children in the non-clinical context of schools does offer a practical way forward, in terms of delivery of such an intervention. There is, to a very great extent, an overlap with the Emotional Well-Being/SEAL curriculum, specifically in the areas of developing self-awareness and emotional intelligence, motivation and social skills. As a tool used regularly and appropriately, mindfulness can increase children's level of self-awareness. It also nurtures their capacity to regulate automatic emotional reactions to events and difficulties that they may encounter on a daily basis in both school and social contexts. There is an increasing evidence base to support its use as an intervention.

Burke's (2010) systematic review of 15 studies was conducted to examine the acceptability and feasibility of mindfulness-based approaches with children and young people between the ages of 4 and 19 years. Harnett and Dawe (2012) looked at 24 pieces of research. These two systematic reviews concluded that the current findings are promising and that mindfulness is accepted by and liked by participants and that there are no apparent adverse effects. Unsurprisingly, considering that this is a new area of research, a number of the pieces of research have been small and/or pilot studies.

The first peer-reviewed controlled study on the delivery of mindfulness in schools was implemented in 2010 by Huppert & Johnson from the Cambridge Well-Being Institute. A four-week syllabus was delivered for use in independent fee-paying boys schools, and in total 173 students were involved in the study. Mindfulness was taught during RE lessons, with each student being in one of 11 classes at the two schools. Six of those classes took normal RE lessons in order to provide a control group for the study, whilst the other five undertook mindfulness training. Initially, the students were required to complete online questionnaires in order to assess their psychological well-being, resilience and reported levels of mindfulness. The measures used include the Warwick Edinburgh Mental Well-being Scale (WEMWBS), the Ego Resiliency Scale and the Cognitive Effective Mindfulness Scale (revised). Overall, it would seem that there was a significant increase in well-being amongst students who received the mindfulness intervention, but of most significance is that those who practised it more regularly reported a greater increase in benefit overall.

Subsequent to the delivery of this study, a further expanded eight-week course was developed and trialled in a number of state schools around the United Kingdom and other European countries. Kuyken et al. (2013) looked at the acceptability and efficacy of the 'Mindfulness in Schools Programme' (MiSP) to enhance mental health and well-being. This non-randomised control trial involved a large participant sample of 522 young people aged between 12 and 16 years, across twelve schools. Teachers were trained by the developers of MiSP and delivered the nine-week programme. This study employed a control group and assessed outcomes at baseline, post-intervention and at a three-month follow up.

The assessment measures employed included Warwick-Edinburgh Mental Well-being Scale (WEMWBS) to look at well-being, Perceived Stress Scale (PSS) and the Center for Epidemiologic Studies Depression Scale (CES-D) to look at mental health, and a brief five question questionnaire to gauge mindfulness practice. In comparing the outcomes between the control group and the intervention group, the researchers found that the MiSP approach had a positive impact on reducing stress, improving well-being and that it had an impact on depressive symptoms.

Napoli, Krech and Holley's (2005) randomised control trial used an integrated mindfulness and relaxation approach as part of the

'Attention Academy Program', which comprised twelve sessions delivered in school. The study looked at 225 children between the ages of 5 and 8 years. The findings showed that children decreased their anxiety, and showed an increase in ability to attend and a reduction in ADHD behaviour (assessed using objective measures of attention).

Semple, Reid and Miller (2005) investigated the feasibility and acceptability of a child-friendly MBCT programme (Mindfulness Based Cognitive Therapy for Children, MBCT-C) for anxious children. This small pilot study involved a six-week programme in one school, attended by 3 boys and 2 girls. They reported an improvement in at least one of three areas: academic performance, anxiety or depressive symptoms and behavioural issues for children as young as seven years.

Schonert-Reichl and Lawlor (2010) examined a mindfulness-based programme run across twelve schools: this involved teachers delivering ten lessons and daily practice three times a day with 246 children. They found a significant increase in positive emotions and optimism with the self-report measures. The teacher report measures indicated a decrease in aggression and oppositional behaviour for the children involved, and an improvement in social and emotional competence.

Joyce et al. (2010) examined a ten-week, teacher-delivered, mindfulness intervention for children between the ages of 10 and 13 years. They identified pre- and post-group differences on measures of behavioural difficulties and depression. There was a significant reduction in self-reported depression scores and behavioural difficulties, especially for those children with clinically significant levels of difficulty before the intervention.

Vickery and Dorjee (2016) of the University of Bangor conducted an eight-week mindfulness programme (Paws b) for 71 children aged from 7 to 9 years old. The programme was delivered by class teachers within the school curriculum. The programme was popular with children, 76 per cent of whom reported 'liking' practising mindfulness at school and many wanting to continue with it. The study showed significantly reduced negative affect and improved metacognition when the programme was followed up after three months. They found that the programme could feasibly be delivered by class teachers as part of the primary school curriculum and have the potential to positively impact on children's emotional well-being.

Growing Evidence for the Positive Effects of Mindfulness Practice for School Staff

A number of recent studies have focused on the use of mindfulness for supporting school staff. One small study examined an eight-week mindfulness-based stress reduction (MBSR) course for two teaching assistants and nine primary school teachers (Gold et al., 2010). They reported the intervention having a positive impact on depression, stress levels, anxiety, self-confidence, sense of pressure, difficulties with planning and problem-solving.

Manas et al. (2011) found a reduction in levels of teacher stress and teacher sick-leave linked to mindfulness training; their research involved a total of 31 secondary school teachers with 15 in the control group and 16 in the experimental group. Compared to the control group, teachers who had the mindfulness training further reported reduced feelings of demotivation, difficulty in coping and pressure. Similarly, Franco et al.'s (2010) larger study found significantly reduced levels of psychological distress in a study of 68 Spanish secondary school teachers, where participants were divided into control and experimental groups. The reduced levels of psychological distress for those teachers in the experimental group were sustained in a follow-up four months later.

A randomised control trial looked at the efficacy of a mindfulness training programme lasting five weeks, for the educators and parents of children with special educational needs (Benn et al., 2012). The research noted that the stress associated with these roles can impact both emotional well-being and also the quality of teaching or parenting. They reported those participants who received the mindfulness training displayed significant reductions in anxiety and stress, as well as increased self-compassion, patience, mindfulness and sense of personal growth. Emotional and relational competence were noted as areas showing improvements relating to measures of empathic concern and forgiveness. A follow-up two months after the study found that these improvements were maintained.

Using Mindfulness in Schools

There have been concerns voiced by some teachers, and also by some parents, that mindfulness training could be perceived as focusing upon within-child deficit features: that is, supporting a general tendency to label young people as having problems that need 'fixing'. However, this is not the intention of the intervention and the majority of practitioners would certainly not see it as being applied in this way. It is vital that mindfulness is not seen as simply part of a therapeutic toolbox. It should instead be firmly centred within the territory of 'flourishing' and within a whole-school approach to positive psychology, which builds upon strengths and builds resilience.

Mindfulness can be seen as an appropriate intervention for use within a nurture group context. Many of our young people who engage in the nurture process and access such provisions will display complex needs, alongside significant attachment difficulties or disorders. It is therefore crucial that they are given opportunities to begin to develop the skills that they will need in order to be able to function more appropriately in both social and learning contexts. On presenting an initiative such as mindfulness to school-based staff, it is important to highlight some of the key aims and outcomes. Using mindfulness techniques with young people and children will, it is hoped, ensure that they can do the following:

- Balance their emotions and lower stress and anger;
- Practise staying calm and focused on learning in the classroom and therefore further develop their skills in both areas;
- Increase the level of trust that they have between themselves and the adults that look after them, and thus make communication easier overall;

- Develop emotional and cognitive understanding and interpersonal awareness and skills;
- Learn how to pay attention: we often say 'pay attention' to children, but we don't actually teach them how to do this;
- Become less reactive and more compassionate to others.

Clearly these are all laudable aims and outcomes, and ones which we would propose for all children within a nurturing context. Further, we would also wish that these children could benefit from:

- Being better able to focus and concentrate;
- Experiencing increased levels of calm;
- Experiencing decreased levels of stress and anxiety;
- Displaying improved impulse control;
- Displaying increased self-awareness;
- Developing natural conflict-resolution skills;
- Developing more empathy and compassion for others;
- Developing and maintaining skilful ways to manage difficult emotions.

So, how does this fit with our overall objective of building resilience and well-being?

Building Resilience & Well-Being

As stated previously, Mindfulness can also support the development of emotional resilience, which is clearly an essential for all children and young people – not just those who are deemed to have been negatively affected by a lack of nurture in the early years. Boosting resilience can help to inoculate against depression and other mental illnesses – it can also build self-confidence and raise achievement. Resilient children can resist adversity, cope with uncertainty and recover more successfully from traumatic events or episodes. Psychologists have long recognised that some children develop well, despite growing up in high-risk environments. This capacity to cope with adversity, and even be strengthened by it, is at the heart of resilience. It is not something that people either have or don't have – resilience is learnable and teachable and as we learn we increase the range of strategies available to us when things get difficult.

Resilience theory has been further influenced in recent years by psychologists working within the field of positive psychology who adopt the position that all aspects of life need to be embraced and that coping with risk and challenge are actually good for us. Stress and adversity are something that we will all experience and it is therefore essential that children learn how to manage such challenges. As Carol Craig, chief executive of the Centre for Confidence and Well-being in Glasgow writes, ‘even with the best care, for children and young people the world can be full of adversity’ (2007, p.92).

Promoting resilience, and the positive sense of self and coping skills that result, is clearly essential within both social and learning environments. Mindfulness approaches can support such an objective as part of a whole-school approach at the individual, group and systems level. It can form one element of such an approach, specifically targeting children who may present as most vulnerable within both the learning and social contexts. It can also be most effective when delivered as part of a whole-school approach to the promotion of mental health and well-being.

Learning & Teaching Mindfulness

As the evidence above shows, mindfulness techniques can have positive impacts for people of all ages. Before thinking about teaching mindfulness in a school or other setting, it is very important that you learn to practise mindfulness yourself. You would not want to be taught to drive by someone who had never been behind the wheel of a car, or learn how to swim from someone who had not been in water.

As with other skills, it is vital to model what you teach; we can only offer what we have developed and learned ourselves. Your role in working with children and young people is more important than any specific mindfulness script or activity and your own practice is central to this. Mindfulness is an ongoing process for all of those who practise it.

You may find it valuable to be honest about your experience as you introduce techniques to the children and young people you are working with, in an appropriate way. For example, telling them if you have found something helpful or noting that this particular activity will be new for you as well and you will be learning together. If you follow such an approach you will notice that the young people respond positively when you share this information and this in turn will help them to feel comfortable about sharing their experiences of their own mindfulness practice as they develop.

As we learn to be mindful we begin, slowly, to develop the ability to notice and attend to our thoughts, feelings and bodily sensations, while also having an awareness of the whole around us. This is developed through ongoing practice. It is important to emphasise that the amount young people practise at home will impact on how they access mindfulness (Weare, 2013).

Issues to Consider

As outlined above, the emerging evidence base for mindfulness suggests that teaching mindfulness to children and young people may have protective benefits, especially in the context of a resiliency-based model. This is especially relevant given the importance of early intervention when working with the emotional well-being of children and young people. No significant adverse effects of mindfulness-based intervention (either practice- or non-practice-based) have been reported (Kostanski & Hassed, 2008).

Nonetheless, it is always important to bear in mind that any therapeutic intervention has the potential to bring to mind personal emotions or experiences that can feel upsetting or overpowering; the introspective aspect of mindfulness practices may evoke difficult feelings or memories (Germer, 2005). Considering the current limited knowledge base, it is recommended that caution be exercised when thinking of adopting mindfulness-based practice approaches for children and young people with significant mental health difficulties: for example, those experiencing active psychoses, suicidal ideation or significant alcohol or substance abuse (Semple & Burke, 2011).

A key consideration is that participation in mindfulness practice be voluntary. Reluctantly practised mindfulness is not mindfulness. Mindfulness requires commitment and cannot be coerced. Thus, when working with children and young-people, the focus should be on introducing the concepts and practices of mindfulness, giving them the opportunities to use them, and ensuring communication is sound. It is suggested that the relationship between the children and young people and their facilitator is the foundation on which these should all rest.

Using this Essential Guide

The Basics

This *Essential Guide* will describe the key elements of mindfulness practice, which can be introduced to children, young people and the adults working with them. These are divided into five sections:

Section One: Activities for Young Children

Section Two: Activities for Adolescents

Section Three: Working with Parents & Carers

Section Four: Working at a Whole-School or Organisational Level

Section Five: Working with Children & Young People with Special Educational Needs (SEN)

Each section will contain practical information about working with that particular group, and ten core activity sessions. Each activity session is generally split into seven parts:

1. Aims
2. Resources
3. Starter activity
4. Main activity
5. End activity
6. Feedback
7. Tips, Ideas & Extensions

The activities have been designed for maximum flexibility for those using them; they can stand alone or can be mixed and matched according to the group interests, needs and motivations.

The activity sessions will last for around 40 minutes in total, but the individual activities can be used in isolation as appropriate. Remember that mindfulness works best when it is habitual and it may therefore make sense to do one short activity every day rather than a 40-minute session once a week.

The activities are flexible, and may be adapted for use with individuals, small groups, or whole classes as appropriate. There is some overlap between the sections and you are encouraged to try out activities from different sections once you are familiar with the principles of mindfulness-based approaches and the needs of your group.

The sessions are intended to be run by adults with an understanding of the philosophy and practice of mindfulness who have experience working with children and young people. These are likely to be therapists, counsellors, teachers, teaching assistants, learning mentors, youth workers and similar.

The main activities in each session will vary, and will be matched to the particular group, but most will be based around the framework shown below in Figure 1.

Figure 1 The Activity Framework

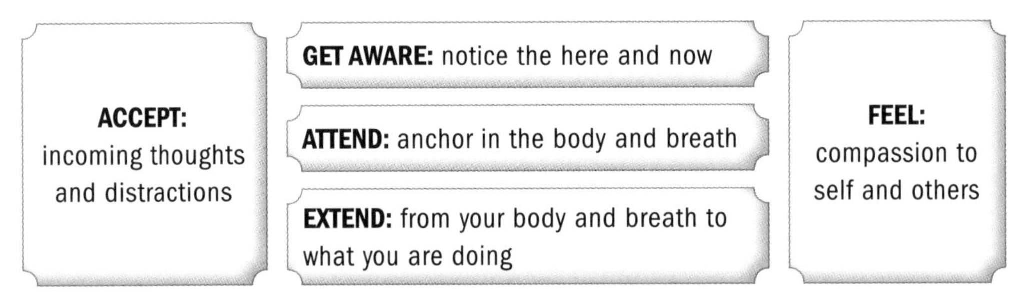

Before You Start

It is suggested that you consider the following key principles for success before you start working with an individual or group of children and young people (CYP):

- **Information:** The young people need to understand what mindfulness is and the kind of things they will be doing and why. They will need time and space to ask questions and have concerns answered.
- **Consent:** Informed consent should be sought from the young people who will be taking part in the sessions, and from their parents or carers. See Resources Templates 1, 2 & 3, 'Information Sheet for Parents & Carers' 'Information Sheet for Young People', and & 'Sample Consent Letter for Parents & Carers'.
- **Motivation:** The young people should want to engage in the activities and the process, or at least to have some curiosity or interest.

- **Containment and relationship:** The young people need to feel supported and emotionally contained by the facilitator before they begin to engage in learning and activities. Think about: introductions, ground rules, non-verbal communication, group size, creating a secure, fun and trusting atmosphere where everyone's ideas matter, listening as well as explaining, not insisting on 'eyes shut', 'lying down', and so on.
- **Skills 1:** The young people must have some body and breath awareness to be able to access the learning and activities.
- **Skills 2:** The young people must have some attentional control to be able to access the learning and activities.
- **Skills 3:** The young people must have sufficiently strong receptive language skills to access the learning and activities.
- **Individual differences:** Before starting work, think about the individuals in your group and try to identify any important factors that should inform your planning, for example, language skills, Special Educational Needs, learning styles.
- **Environment:** Consider the room in which you will be working, including background noise and lighting. A quiet, private room, dimly lit is ideal, but will seldom be available in a school environment. Preferably there should be room for individuals to have space around them for listening to the mindfulness scripts, whether seated or lying on the floor.
- **Time:** Think about using a timer to maintain the structure and pace of your sessions.
- **Involving the children or young people:** To help to embed mindfulness practice, it is useful to bring the young people into the process. There are a number of different ways to do this, for example, at each session a different child or group could have responsibility for getting the resources, or for reminding everyone of the start time before the session.
- **Start slow:** Plan to start with a short, clear activity involving breath.

- **Involvement and control:** Try to build in processes that encourage the young people to be actively involved in their learning and to reflect on it, for example: peer discussion work; personal sticker charts; personal mindfulness records (see Resources Template 4, 'Personal Mindfulness Record'); letter-writing or video-making activities, so that they can share their skills with others; and opportunities to talk in assembly or to small groups about their learning and skills.
- **Feedback:** Ask how the session went afterwards; listen to this feedback and act on it.
- **Record and reflect:** Think about noting down very briefly any reflections or action points for your next session, so as to extend your learning as well as that of your group.
- **Practise! Practise! Practise!** Integrating mindfulness practice into the regular school or group routine, even for just a minute or two, will help it to become part of the culture. In schools, finding a regular time to hold the session, for example when the children have come back into the classroom after lunch, will help with this.
- **Back-Up:** Consider in every session how to encourage generalisation of the skills learnt beyond the group, for example: take away tasks, diaries, communication across the school and with home, inviting visitors to the group.

Using Mindfulness Scripts

Some of the activities in this *Essential Guide* involve 'Mindfulness (or Meditation) Scripts'. A Mindfulness Script is simply a few paragraphs of text that can be read aloud to facilitate meditation. Scripts can be useful with a range of groups, from young children to young adults. Table 1, below, provides an overview of the age-group suitability of the nine Mindfulness Scripts you will find in the Resources section of this *Essential Guide*. The Scripts can be used individually, in small groups, or in larger whole groups. It is important to match the script to the individual or group you are working with. A selection of these Scripts could be made into a booklet to give both to young people and to those working with them.

A few guiding principles when using the Scripts:

- Children under the age of ten are unlikely to maintain attention on a script for more than a minute.
- Think about the language you are using in your script and the developmental level, attentional skills, and motivations, of your group.
- Young children are likely to respond best to scripts which include obvious reference to the senses and the body.

General Tips for Using Mindfulness or Meditation Scripts

Make sure the individual or group knows what to expect before starting the meditation. 'Meditation' can seem threatening and even silly to some people, and this should be considered. It is worth discussing potential hopes and fears with the group before starting the first activity, as well as offering the opportunity to ask questions. You could show a short video clip to help to set the scene. The following tips can help you to achieve the best possible setting and results:

- Think about calling the activity something other than meditation, for example: 'Relaxation', 'Guided Visualisation', 'Awareness Time', 'Sense Connect', 'Now Be'.

- Do not insist that people close their eyes, as this can be frightening or threatening for adults and children alike. Offer alternatives, for example: head in hands, eyes looking down, find a corner, focus on a spot on the wall. Think about having some flight eye-masks available for those who want them.
- These activities are likely to work best if the group facilitator has a strong and trusting relationship with the individual or group.
- It is good idea to establish a few agreed and understood simple ground rules before starting the first script, to ensure people feel at ease and confident within the group.
- Consider making meditations optional, particularly with older groups. These kinds of activities are likely to be most effective with small (around six to ten), stable, motivated groups rather than whole-class or staff groups.
- Facilitators should try to find the time to practise reading from the script before they do it for real! Think about tone of voice. Use a timer and remember to pause and to speak slowly.
- Ask the group how they found the activity and try to attend to their feedback. One way to do this is to ask each person to write down one word to sum up their experience and put it in an envelope on their way out. You could also ask people to rate their experience on a scale.
- When introducing a script for the first time, try to keep it short and breath-focused.
- Encourage group members to practise on a daily basis at home, perhaps starting with one minute of breath-awareness a day, at a set time. Try pairing group members up and giving them 5 minutes at the end of a session to tell each other when and how they plan to practise at home, and ask them to record their reaction on a scale, as in the diagram below.

Table 1: An Overview of the Mindfulness Scripts and Suggested Uses
Suitable for: YC = Young Children; YP = Adolescent; A = Adult

Script Number & Title	Who for?	Script Number
1 Mini-Script A short mindfulness script used in the first section of this book 'Activities for Young Children'; suitable for use with the youngest members of a group learning the new technique of mindfulness.	YC	1
2 Introduction to Meditation This is a good introduction, as it begins to raise sensory awareness very simply – by focusing on the breath. The breath is a useful focus, because it reminds us that we are in the present ('this is what is happening now') and because it connects us to our senses and how we feel.	YC YP A	2
3 Mindful Mouthful This is about savouring food, while using all the senses.	YC YP A	3
4 Progressive Muscle Relaxation This works on drawing awareness to the present experience of the body and learning to consciously scan it and relax it, part by part. It is good for relieving tension and worry.	YP A	4
5 Full Body Scan This raises sensory and bodily awareness through a whole body 'scan'. A shortened version of this script is included in Activity 2.1.	YP A	5
6 Mindful Listening This script helps to focus on the here and now, rather than the past.	YP A	6
7 Mindful Looking This script is about noticing nature in the present and looking mindfully at what is around us.	YC YP A	7
8 Mindful Movement This script raises body awareness and encourages gratitude and acceptance.	YP A	8
9 Kindness & Gratitude This script starts with a short body scan and moves to a focus on love, kindness and gratitude towards ourselves and others.	YP A	9

Note: Please be aware of the individuals you are working with and adapt these scripts accordingly, for example, by simplifying the language or shortening their duration.

1

Activities for Young Children

Background

As discussed previously, Mindfulness requires the intentional awareness of 'being'. Whilst young children are frequently 'in the moment', their awareness of this develops over time and requires a degree of attentional control and self-awareness. Very young children do not possess this. Without the capacity to 'pay attention, in the moment, on purpose, non-judgementally' (even if briefly), young children are unlikely to be suitable for mindfulness interventions.

It is suggested that at around seven years of age, most children have the cognitive capacity to access age-appropriate mindfulness activities, such as those in this section. However, there will clearly be individual differences, and numerous other factors of relevance when considering who to include in a mindfulness group or individual intervention. Some of these factors are shown in Figure 2 and are worth considering when setting up your group. The Resources Template 5 is a five-question, 'Brief Screening Tool for Young Children'.

As with all sections in this *Essential Guide*, the activities need not be run in order and do not form part of a progressive programme, as such. They can stand alone or can be mixed and matched to fit group or timetable requirements.

The majority of the activities in this section have a concrete sensory focus and are suitable for children aged from 7 to 11 years (Key Stage Two: Years 3–6) who have been identified as receptive, when asked the questions in Resources Template 5: 'Brief Screening Tool for Young Children'. This includes those across the ability range, with SEN, poor attendance, or who sometimes struggle to concentrate. Section 5 contains further information on the adaptation of activities for use with children with SEN.

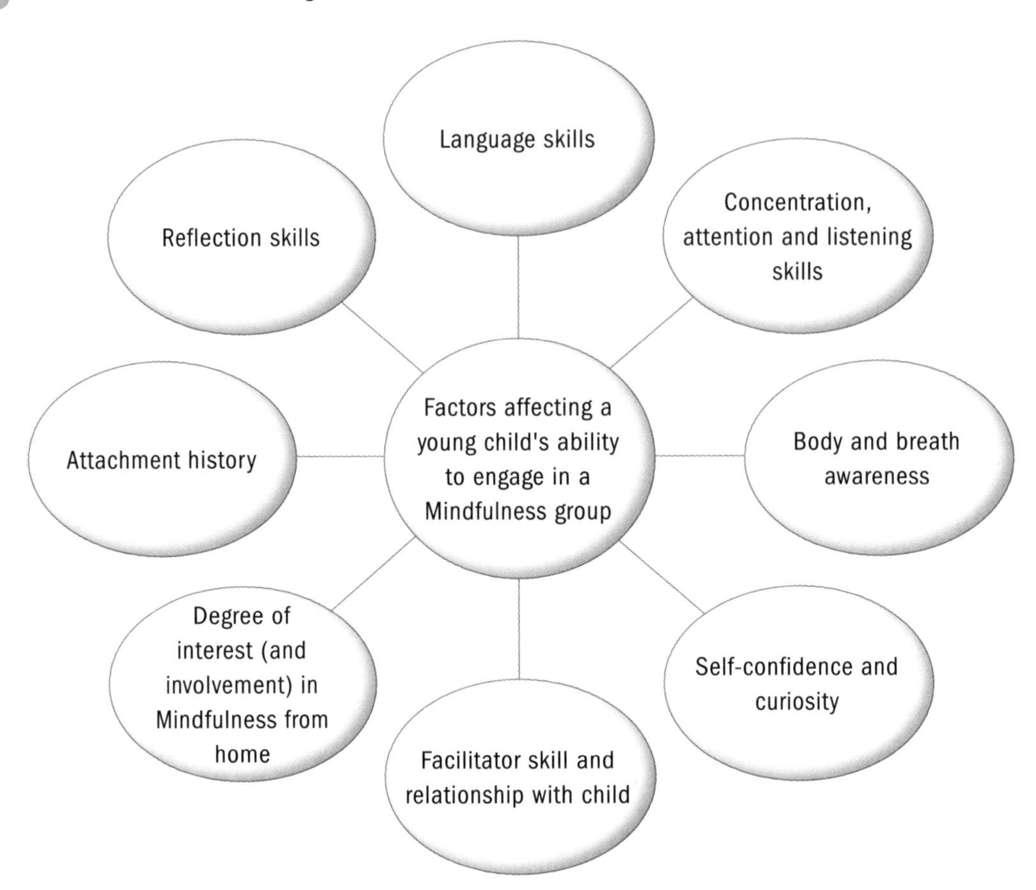

Figure 2: Factors Affecting a Young Child's Suitability for a Mindfulness Group

1.1 Favourite Place

Aims

- To increase awareness of the breath.
- To create a mental image of a relaxing place.

Resources

Worksheet 1, 'Mindful Breathing', and Worksheet 2, 'Favourite Place', one for each group member; selection of photographs and images, glue, scissors, paper, pens, magazines and newspapers, computer access as appropriate.

Starter Activity

Explain and carry out the 'Mindful Breathing' exercise (Worksheet 1).

Main Activity

1. Explain that mindful breathing can be useful to calm us down and to help us experience what is happening now, rather than thinking about what has happened in the past or what might happen in the future. Explain the aims of the session.
2. Introduce the 'Favourite Place' activity (Worksheet 2) as another way to help us relax: today we are going to make a picture of our favourite place on a piece of paper and then try to put it into our heads.
3. The children can use pictures provided to make their images.
4. When children have made their images, allow 10 minutes for them to join with a partner and share their ideas. Ask them to think of three words for their partner's image to share with the group.

End Activity

1. Repeat the 'Mindful Breathing' activity.
2. Ask everyone to close their eyes and imagine their favourite place in their minds, including all of the details and how they feel. What can you see? Smell? Hear? Touch?

Feedback

Talk to a partner about how you found today's session, including which mindful breathing session was better and why? When and why might you use the favourite place image in your head? How can you try not to forget it?

page 1 of 2

1.1 Favourite Place

Tips, Ideas & Extensions

You could create a display or gallery of favourite places; the children's images could be included in a circle-time activity; play a 'guess the place' game, when one child describes their favourite place and the group have to guess which picture matches it; encourage children to take their picture (or a photograph of it) home to show family and friends; in the next session ask the children to shut their eyes and imagine their favourite place as a starter activity; ask children to feedback situations when they have used the favourite place image in their heads.

1.2 Feet in Jelly

Aims

- To increase awareness of the breath.
- To increase awareness of sensory input.

Resources

Worksheet 3, 'Floating Balloon', and Worksheet 1, 'Mindful Breathing'. Big plastic bags; jelly; spoons; access to soap, water and towels; blindfolds; washing-up bowls.

Starter Activity

Explain and carry out the 'Floating Balloon' activity (Worksheet 3)

Main Activity

1. Discuss the 'Floating Balloon' activity and the idea that we can get 'in tune' with our bodies moment by moment. Explain the aims of the session.
2. How can we 'tune in'? Brainstorm ways to 'tune in' or notice our bodies and feelings. Discuss these ideas.
3. As a group, list or draw the five senses and link these to 'getting in tune'.
4. Now focus on our sense of touch. Form pairs and work with a partner. Everyone should have bare feet. Sitting close to each other, each partner in turn closes their eyes, while looking down or staring ahead, and their partner helps them to put their feet into the bag of jelly. When everyone has their feet in the bags of jelly, read the following to the group:

Be still and quiet. Focus your attention on your feet and how they feel right now. Really concentrate on them. The toes. The heels. The ankles. The top of the foot. The left foot. The right foot. Wiggle your toes slightly and be aware of how your toes feel right now. Don't worry if you start thinking of something else – just bring your attention back to your feet. Now slowly start to notice the sounds and activities around you and open your eyes.

End Activity

Worksheet 1, 'Mindful Breathing'.

1.2 Feet in Jelly

Feedback

How was the activity? What was the point of it? As a group identify what everyone has learned today, referring back to the aims of the session. Now form pairs again and talk to a partner about how you personally found today's session: What went well? What will change?

Tips, Ideas & Extensions

Try a range of other sensory activities, for example, feet in ice, walking on popcorn, or pepper in a bag. Space and literacy levels permitting, try getting the children to read the 'Be still and quiet' from the Main Activity script to each other in pairs.

1.3 What's in the Bag?

Aims

- To increase awareness of the breath.
- To increase sensory awareness.

Resources

Worksheet 1, 'Mindful Breathing', and Worksheet 3, 'Floating Balloon'; Script 1, 'Mini-Script' (one for each person). Three bags of different items – anything goes, but try to include a range of textures, shapes and, if possible, temperatures, for example: chalk, tin foil, peeled grapes, polystyrene, bubble wrap, small soft toy, an ice pack, or blindfolds.

Starter Activity

Explain and carry out the 'Mindful Breathing' exercise (Worksheet 1).

Main Activity

1. Discuss the 'Floating Balloon' activity from the last session, and link this to the idea of being aware of our bodies and our breath, and how this might help us relax. Explain the aims of the session.
2. Separate the group into three smaller groups and give them a bag each. Within small groups everyone should have a partner. In pairs, take it in turns to shut your eyes, put your hand in the bag and pick an object while your partner reads from the 'Mini-Script' (Script 1).

End Activity

'Floating Balloon' (Worksheet 3)

Feedback

Draw a picture of how you felt during the 'Floating Balloon' exercise. Share pictures with a partner.

Tips, Ideas & Extensions

Invite the group to make up their own sensory bags. Help the group to learn the 'Mini-Script' by heart and discuss why this might be helpful.

1.4 Mindful Colouring

Aims

- To increase awareness of the breath.
- To attend in the present moment.

Resources

Worksheet 3, 'Floating Balloon', Worksheet 4, 'Mindful Colouring', Worksheet 1, 'Mindful Breathing', and Worksheet 5, 'Mazes' (one for each person). A range of colouring sheets and books, coloured pens and pencils, relaxing music.

Starter Activity

Explain and carry out the 'Floating Balloon' activity (Worksheet 3).

Main Activity

1. Ask everyone to think about how easy or hard they found it to pay attention in the moment during 'Floating Balloon'. They shouldn't worry about how easy or hard it was, just notice.
2. Discuss examples of when people have paid attention in the present moment. When is it easy and when is it difficult to do this?
3. Explain the aims of the session and the meaning of the word 'Mindfulness' (it is about paying attention, on purpose, in the moment, non-judgementally). Explain that today we are going to try to be mindful while colouring in.
4. Read the guidance notes from Worksheet 4, 'Mindful Colouring' while the group draw and colour their pictures.

End Activity

'Mindful Breathing' (Worksheet 1). Remember to try to pay attention in the present moment, without judging.

Feedback

How was the activity? Discuss with partners the difference between colouring and 'mindful' colouring? What is the point of being mindful?

1.4 Mindful Colouring

Tips, Ideas & Extensions

Try colouring in silence or colouring with music playing; ask the group to design their own colouring sheets and share them with each other. Try using 'Mazes' (Worksheet 5) or newspaper circling: take a large sheet of newspaper and some colouring pens. Circle words or letters in different places on the sheet to make patterns.

1.5 Sounds of Nature

Aims

- To increase awareness of the breath.
- To increase sensory awareness.
- To maintain attention in the present for a few minutes.

Resources

Worksheet 6, 'Peaceful River', Worksheet 7, 'Sounds of Nature', and Worksheet 1, 'Mindful Breathing'. Access to outside space, means of recording sounds.

Starter Activity

Explain and carry out the 'Peaceful River' exercise (Worksheet 6).

Main Activity

1. How did you find the 'Peaceful River' exercise?
2. Explain the aims of the session and that you will be going out and about to do some mindful listening (that is, paying attention to what we hear, on purpose, in the moment, without judgement).
3. As a group go out and listen to the sounds around you: use Worksheet 7, 'Sounds of Nature', for guidance.

End Activity

'Mindful Breathing' (Worksheet 1).

Feedback

How did today's session make you feel? Brainstorm feelings on a big sheet of paper or whiteboard and discuss in the whole group.

Tips, Ideas & Extensions

Ask the group to list as many of the sounds that they heard as they can remember. They could also sit quietly and try to remember other sensory information – what did they see, smell and touch? How did they feel? The children could record the sounds they hear while out and about and play these back to the group. Discuss how these recordings might be used and which sounds people find most relaxing and why.

1.6 Mindful Mouth

Aims

- To pay attention in the moment to a range of sensory information.

Resources

Worksheet 1, 'Mindful Breathing', and Worksheet 6, 'Peaceful River'; Script 3, 'Mindful Mouthful'. Different foods (e.g., raisins, crisps, celery, cottage cheese, chocolate), spoons, paper plates. Set up an area for each food with chairs nearby.

Note: *Be aware of food allergies and preferences and be aware of food hygiene.*

Starter Activity

Explain and carry out the 'Mindful Breathing' exercise (Worksheet 1).

Main Activity

1. Explain the aims and the plan for the session.
2. List and/or draw the five senses on the board or a big sheet of paper. Discuss the idea that our senses are there to keep us alive, but that for a lot of the time we don't pay much attention to them. Today we are going to *tune in* to all five senses.
3. Each person picks an area and helps themselves to a small amount of that food. Now read to the group from Script 3, 'Mindful Mouthful'. If time permits, move to different food areas and repeat the exercise.

End Activity

'Peaceful River' exercise (Worksheet 6).

Feedback

With a partner discuss: Why did we do this activity? Which food did you like best and why? Was this session just about the sense of taste? Feedback thought and ideas to the whole group.

Tips, Ideas & Extensions

Try different foods; try sensing in the dark or with an eye mask on; play a game of guess the food. Consider including some challenging foods, for example, (mild) chillies or clove powder (ensure you first have the agreement of each group member). Start thinking about connecting senses and feelings, for example: how did you feel before, during and after eating the chilli?

1.7 Lungs

Aims

- To raise awareness of the breath.
- To extend the out-breath, so as to aid relaxation.

Resources

Worksheet 1, 'Mindful Breathing', and Worksheet 8, 'Soaking Up Sunshine'. Large empty plastic flask, washing-up bowls, rubber tubing, access to a tap, food colouring, timers, straws.

Note: *Be aware that children should not hold their breath or breathe in or out for longer than is comfortable. Remind them that this is not a competition. Encourage them to be aware of how their body and breath feel and to respond to this, rather than simply following your instructions. During the water breath activity, remind them to breathe out and not in through the water!*

Starter Activity

Explain and carry out the 'Mindful Breathing' exercise (Worksheet 1).

Main Activity

1. Discuss the length of the in-breath versus the length of the out-breath in relation to the 'Mindful Breathing' exercise they have just done. Explain that some people find lengthening their out-breath helps them to relax.
2. Ask the group to try breathing in for 3 seconds and then out for 5 seconds with their eyes shut. Remind them that they should attend to their own breath and only hold their in- or out-breath for as long as is comfortable.
3. Try breathing out through water, using a straw. It can be fun to colour the water with food colouring.

End Activity

'Soaking Up Sunshine' (Worksheet 8).

Feedback

How was today's session? How easy is it to be aware of the breath? What happens if other thoughts push in?

page 1 of 2

1.7 Lungs

Tips, Ideas & Extensions

Try breathing in and out while watching a clock and counting in seconds or while looking closely at a candle flame, picture or pattern. If children seem to understand the concept of the straw-breathing activity, think about extending it so they breathe out down a rubber tube or straw into an inverted container filled with water. They can then see the level of the water go down as they breathe out. Ask them to focus on this and attend to their own breath in the moment.

1.8 Identifying Personal Relaxation Strategies: a Circus

Aims

- To increase awareness of the breath.
- To identify mindful relaxation strategies that suit each person.

Resources

Worksheet 3, 'Floating Balloon'; Worksheet 9, 'Cards for Relaxation Zones' printed on to large (A2-sized if possible) sheets of paper; one copy of Worksheet 10, 'Personal Relaxation Grid', for each person; Worksheet 11, 'Relaxation Strategies', one for each person; Worksheet 1, 'Mindful Breathing'.

In advance of the session create three different relaxation zones: the 'Light Area', a black-out sensory tent, or similar, with coloured light projectors or other sensory lights inside; the 'Soft Area', a sectioned-off corner or space under a table with a soft cloth thrown over it, full of soft blankets, cushions, and so forth; the 'Music Area', comfortable cushions or seats with two iPods (and headphones for each), containing a selection of music.

Starter Activity

'Floating Balloon' (Worksheet 3).

Main Activity

Working in pairs, each pair spends 10 minutes in each of the three relaxation zones in the room, following the guidelines on the cards. After each 10-minute session they can fill in their 'Personal Relaxation Grid' and compare their personal response to each area. Extension: in pairs, look at Worksheet 11, 'Relaxation Strategies', and try some of these out. Record how they went on the 'Personal Relaxation Grid'.

End Activity

'Mindful Breathing' (Worksheet 1).

Feedback

With a partner compare your Personal Relaxation Grids and discuss how you will use them in the future and what you have learned about yourself today.

page 1 of 2

1.8 Identifying Personal Relaxation Strategies: a Circus

Tips, Ideas & Extensions

This session works best with a group of six split into three pairs, but could be adapted to a larger group if there is enough space and resources allow. Extend the session by asking children to design their own personal relaxation zone or activity – money, time and space are no object!

1.9 Acceptance

Aims

- To recognise and accept that we feel different emotions, that emotions pass and need not be overwhelming.

Resources

Worksheet 3, 'Floating Balloon'. Create envelopes for each group member containing copies of the four pictures on Worksheet 12, 'Bears with Feelings' (sad, happy, worried, angry); Worksheet 1, 'Mindful Breathing'.

Starter Activity

Explain and carry out the 'Floating Balloon' exercise (Worksheet 3).

Main Activity

1. Explain the aim and plan for the session.
2. Children open their envelopes and choose a bear to match best how they feel right now.
3. Ask the children to direct their attention to this emotion and stick with it. Really think about how it feels to be sad/angry/happy/worried. Imagine your bear is sitting near you or on your lap. Accept your bear. This is what being sad/angry/happy/worried feels like.

End Activity

'Mindful Breathing' (Worksheet 1).

Feedback

Close your eyes and describe a 'feelings bear' to a partner. They have to try to guess what this feeling might be called.

Tips, Ideas & Extensions

If appropriate, you could ask the group to move around the room to stand next to large pictures of the bears. Try using photographs of people or pictures of emojis instead of bears; if you think the children have the capacity, and have engaged well, ask them to try out the different bears (emotions) and to notice how they feel. Ask the children to notice when they 'meet these bears' or feel these feelings over the course of each day. Talk to them about: how long the bear was with them; how it felt; whether it was it easy to accept the bear; and how different bears feel differently.

1.10 My Mindful Garden

Aims

Note: *This could be a project or a stand-alone session.*

- To increase sensory awareness.
- To begin to recognise a feeling of compassion towards oneself and others.

Resources

'Soaking Up Sunshine' (Worksheet 8). Access to an outside space, bag of soil, trowels, watering cans or plastic cups, selection of seeds, small plant pots, a window box or similar, string, plant markers, stickers and pens.

Starter Activity

'Soaking Up Sunshine' (Worksheet 8).

Main Activity

1. If your eyes are shut, keep them shut. Keep your concentration. Imagine a perfect garden. Pay attention to all of its detail: what you see; what you smell; what you hear; what you touch. How does it feel to be in this garden? Don't worry if other thoughts pop into your head, notice them and calmly return to thinking about your garden. Now slowly become aware of your surroundings again and open your eyes.
2. Planting activity: each child selects a few seeds, fills their pots with soil, plants their seeds, adds some water and labels their pots.

End Activity

Imagine your perfect garden again. Imagine the seeds you have planted today sitting in their pots and slowly, slowly, starting to grow. How does this make you feel? Recognise this feeling and give it a name or colour in your head.

Feedback

Draw a picture of your garden and show it to a partner. How did you find the session today?

Tips, Ideas & Extensions

This could become a project over weeks or months if you decide to design and grow your own garden, window box or pot.

2

Activities for Adolescents

Be aware that a number of the starter activities in this section involve a 'body scan' activity. It is strongly recommended that the first session you do with an individual or group introduces this concept and allows the young people to familiarise themselves with the concept.

2.1 Body Scan

Aims

- To raise sensory and bodily awareness.

Resources

Script 5, 'Full Body Scan', one for each person.

Introduction

Explain to the group that they are going to learn to do a body scan.

Ask everyone to sit comfortably: this might be sitting or lying on the floor, or with their head on the desk.

Explain that this might feel like a weird or unusual activity, but that they should just give it a try. Explain that the point of the activity is to help with self-awareness and relaxation. Even though it might feel strange at first, lots of people find it helpful so they are encouraged to have a go.

The first time you introduce this activity, it would be best to use the short version of the script and then build up to using the longer version.

Once everyone is comfortable, read out the script from Script 5; copies can be given to group members so they can practise in their own time.

Short or Introductory Version

Start by focusing on the breath. Feel your breath entering and leaving your body. Notice how it feels. Really focus on this feeling. If thoughts pop into your head or your mind wanders, notice this and refocus on your breathing. Notice the in-breath and the out-breath. In ... out ...

Next take your full attention to your feet. Feel their contact with the ground.

Next take your full attention to the backs of your legs ...

Next move all your attention slowly up your spine. Try to sense each vertebra ... Move up the back to the shoulder blades. PAUSE. Think about how they feel right now ... tight? ... relaxed?

Next bring all your attention to your face. Bring your attention back to the here and now and your breath if your mind wanders. PAUSE. When you are ready, slowly open your eyes ...

page 1 of 2

2.1 Body Scan

Longer Version

Start by focusing on the breath. Feel your breath entering and leaving your body. Notice how it feels. Really focus on this feeling. If thoughts pop into your head or your mind wanders, notice this without judgement and refocus on your breathing. Notice the in-breath and the out-breath. In ... out ...

Next take your full attention to the soles of your feet. Feel their contact with the ground. Can you feel the contact between the bottom of your feet and your shoes? PAUSE. Feel for tightness, heat, cold, movement. Concentrate fully on your feet ... now ... in the present moment. It is likely that your mind will wander off to other places, but keep bringing it back to your feet ... the soles of your feet. PAUSE. Notice the thoughts that flit in and then bring your attention back to your feet. PAUSE.

Next take your full attention to the backs of your legs ... your ankles ... your calves ... the back of each knee in turn ... the back of your heels. Maybe you have never attended to the back of your heels before. Really attend to how they feel. PAUSE.

Now bring your full attention to the front of your knees. Are they touching your clothing or are they exposed to the air? Or are they touching the table? PAUSE.

Consciously explore your contact with your chair. Think about how this feels. If thoughts come into your head, gently notice them and push them away.

Next move all your attention slowly up your spine. Try to sense each vertebra ... Can you feel your vertebrae? If you cannot, acknowledge this without judgement and steadily return your attention to your back. Move up the back to the shoulder blades. PAUSE. Think about how they feel right now ... tight? ... relaxed? ... warm? PAUSE. Think about how they feel to you right now.

Now move your full attention round to the front. Notice your stomach and chest. Can you feel any movement in the stomach? Can you feel any tightness in your chest?

Next bring all your attention to your face. Think about how it feels. Any tension? ... hot? ... cold? Attend to your nose ... eyes ... lips ... cheeks ... forehead ... ears ... PAUSE. Bring your attention back to the here and now and your bodily experiences if your mind wanders. PAUSE. When you are ready, slowly open your eyes ...

2.2 Habits & Scripts

Aims

- To introduce the idea of relaxation, using a script.

Resources

Worksheet 6, 'Peaceful River'; pens and paper.

Starter Activity

A habit is something you do all the time, without really thinking about it. List three habits or habitual emotional responses that you have, which you think might not be helpful. List three thoughts or emotions that sometimes whizz around your head, and which you find it hard to switch off. This swirling cycle, which can be quite emotional, is called rumination and it can be tiring and unhelpful. Meditation can help us control it because it helps focus our minds.

Main Activity

Once the group are settled, slowly read the following script:

Sit comfortably and at rest. Your eyes can be open or closed. Listen to your breath. Feel your natural breath. With me: breathe in and count. When you are ready, count in your head at the same time as breathing out. Let's repeat. Count in ... Count out ...

End Activity

'Peaceful River' (Worksheet 6).

Feedback

With a partner discuss how you found today's session and what you might use in the future. Revisit the habits you identified in the Starter Activity and think again about how you might try to break them.

Tips, Ideas & Extensions

Vary the meditation script used in the Main Activity by selecting one from the examples in Mindfulness Scripts 2–9, or create your own script. See the Introduction for information on how to select and use the scripts.

2.3 Letter to Myself

Aims

- To write a letter to your future self.

Resources

Script 5, 'Full Body Scan'; Worksheet 1, 'Mindful Breathing'; pens, paper and envelopes.

Starter Activity

Script 5, 'Full Body Scan'.

Main Activity

Write a letter to your future self. Once your letter is written, you will be putting it away in a drawer or cupboard for at least six months – a good idea is to pick somewhere you would need to clear out when you move, but not for at least six months.

Take paper and a pen and begin to think about what you will want to say to yourself in six or twelve months' time. Ask yourself:

- Who am I today?
- What are my goals? What are my dreams?
- What makes me happy?
- What makes me unhappy?
- What am I struggling with?

Then think about where you hope to be in six or twelve months' time:

- Where will I be then?
- What will my hopes and goals be then?
- What will I have achieved?
- Where will I have focused my effort and energy?
- What/who makes me happy?
- What did I used to struggle with, but don't anymore?

Next write about all of the great things that you have in your life. Remind your future self of the things in your life that make you happy. You might write about your hobbies, your interests, your friends, your pets, your family – whatever you feel is important. Write this so that in six or twelve months' time you do not forget to reflect on the special things in your life now.

Now, hide the letter in a safe place.

2.3 Letter to Myself

End Activity

1. Do the 'Mindful Breathing' exercise (Worksheet 1).
2. Close your eyes and imagine your favourite place in your mind, including all the details and how you feel. What can you see? Smell? Hear? Touch?

Feedback

Reflect on this activity – did anything that you thought about or wrote surprise you? How do you think it will be when you read this letter in six or twelve months?

Tips, Ideas & Extensions

You could collect in the sealed envelopes after the letters have been written and store them in a safe place.

2.4 Relaxation Strategies

Aims

- To identify mindful relaxation strategies that suit you.

Resources

Set of three A2 cards, one for each relaxation zone, made using Worksheet 9, 'Cards for Relaxation Zones'; Worksheet 10, 'Personal Relaxation Grid' (one per person), and Worksheet 11, 'Relaxation Strategies' (one per person). In advance of the session create three different relaxation zones: the 'Light Area', a black-out sensory tent, or similar, with coloured light projectors or other sensory lights inside; the 'Soft Area', a sectioned-off corner or space under a table with a soft cloth thrown over it, full of soft blankets, cushions, and so forth; the 'Music Area', comfortable cushions or seats with two iPods (and headphones for each), containing a selection of music.

Starter Activity

On your own, brainstorm all the things that you do to help you relax. Now join with a partner to compare your ideas.

Main Activity

In pairs, young people spend 10 minutes in each of the three relaxation zones in the room in silence. They fill in their Personal Relaxation Grid (Worksheet 10), which compares their personal response to each zone. Extension: Working in pairs, have a look at Worksheet 11, 'Relaxation Strategies', and try some of these out. Record how they went on your Personal Relaxation Grid.

End Activity

Worksheet 1, 'Mindful Breathing'.

Feedback

With your partner compare your Personal Relaxation Grids and discuss how you will use them in the future and what you have learnt about yourself today. Which was your favourite relaxation strategy? Does everyone relax in the same way?

2.4 Relaxation Strategies

Tips, Ideas & Extensions

This session works best with a group of six split into three pairs, but could be adapted to a bigger group if there is enough space and if resources allow (e.g., iPods). Zones will need to be set up in advance of the young people's arrival and should take into account the needs and vulnerabilities of the group. Extend this session by asking children to design their own personal relaxation zone or activity (money, time and space no object).

2.5 Suitcase

Aims

- To be mindful of the people, places, things and ideas that are important to us.

Resources

Script 5, 'Full Body Scan'; Worksheet 13, 'Suitcase'; plain paper, pens, pictures, computer access as appropriate.

Starter Activity

Script 5, 'Full Body Scan'.

Main Activity

Explain the session aim. Give out Worksheet 13, 'Suitcase', and read it through. Young people then work on their suitcase independently.

End Activity

In silence (eyes shut, if you are comfortable to do this) take a few minutes to think about who you would like to show your suitcase to and why.

Feedback

Talk to a partner about how you found today's session. If you are happy to do so, share your suitcase sheet and ideas with a partner and talk it through.

Tips, Ideas & Extensions

Think about extending this to explore young people's ideas about what is positive and important to them, for example, by making video clips showing 'I am ...', 'I can ...', 'I have ...' statements and displays.

2.6 Pleasant Events Calendar

Aims

- To notice and explore positive events in everyday life.

Resources

Worksheet 14, 'Pleasant Events Calendar' (one for each person), and Worksheet 1, 'Mindful Breathing'.

Starter Activity

A habit is something you do all the time, without really thinking about it. Sometimes our habits can be difficult and not helpful. Other times we have positive habits or habitual emotional responses. We are going to notice some of these positive moments. List three everyday pleasant, positive events that have happened for you in the last week. You might be able to think of more than three!

Main Activity

Once you have identified three pleasant events from the last week, give each young person a copy of Worksheet 14, 'Pleasant Events Calendar'. They each fill in their own calendar for the three pleasant events they identified.

End Activity

Worksheet 1, 'Mindful Breathing'.

Feedback

Talk to a partner about how you found today's session. If you are happy to, share something from your group with them.

Tips, Ideas & Extensions

The young people take the calendar away with them and see if they can notice one pleasant event for each day of the week and record it.

2.7 Favourite Place

Aims

- To increase awareness of the breath.
- To create a mental image of a relaxing place.

Resources

Script 5, 'Full Body Scan'; Worksheet 2, 'Favourite Place', and Worksheet 1, 'Mindful Breathing'; selection of photographs and images, glue, scissors, paper, pens, magazines and newspapers, computer access as appropriate.

Starter Activity

Script 5, 'Full Body Scan'.

Main Activity

1 Explain that mindful breathing can be useful to calm us down and to help us experience what is happening *now* rather than thinking about what happened in the past or might happen in the future. Explain the aims.

2 Introduce the 'Favourite Place' activity (Worksheet 2) as another way to help us relax: 'Today we are going to make a picture of our favourite place on a piece of paper and then try to put it into our heads.'

3 Young people create their images.

4 When young people have made their images allow 10 minutes for them to join with a partner and share them. Ask them to think of three words for their partner's image to share with the class.

End Activity

Use Worksheet 1, 'Mindful Breathing'. 2. Close your eyes and imagine your favourite place in your mind, including all the details and how you feel. What can you see? Smell? Hear? Touch?

Feedback

Talk to a partner about how you found today's session, including which mindful breathing session was better and why? When and why might you use the favourite place image in your head? How can you try not to forget it?

2.7 Favourite Place

Tips, Ideas & Extensions

Think about putting up a display or 'gallery'; think about playing a 'guess the place' game, when one young person describes their favourite place and the group have to guess which picture matches it; encourage young people to take their picture home (or a photograph of it) to show to family and friends; in the next session think about asking young people to shut their eyes and imagine their favourite place as a starter activity; ask young people to feedback situations when they have used the favourite place image in their heads.

2.8 Acceptance

Aims

- To recognise and accept that we feel different emotions, that emotions pass, and that they need not be overwhelming.

Resources

Script 5, 'Full Body Scan'. Using Worksheet 15, 'Weather Pictures', prepare envelopes containing a selection of pictures of weather.

Starter Activity

Script 5, 'Full Body Scan'.

Main Activity

1 Explain the aim and plan for the session.

2 Young people open their envelopes and choose a weather card to match how they feel now.

3 Ask them to look closely at the card and attend to how they feel right now. Tell them to direct their attention to this emotion and stick with it. Now move your attention away from this emotion and reset your attention on the room you are in.

4 Talk to a partner about how you found the activity.

End Activity

Focus on your breath. In. Out. Now imagine a cloudy sky. Look at the clouds moving across it. Start to feel the sun on your face, very gently. Watch closely as the clouds move slowly apart and away ... and the sun comes out. Feel the sun on your face and look up at the clear blue sky.

Discuss as a group the idea that emotions can come and go and need not be overwhelming. How can we raise awareness of our feelings as we go about our busy lives? How can we help them not be overwhelming?

Feedback

Why might it be helpful to pay close attention to how we feel? Is it always helpful? What did you think of thinking about feelings by thinking about weather? How else could we do this task? (Colour? Faces? Cartoons?)

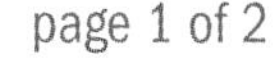

2.8 Acceptance

Tips, Ideas & Extensions

Think about asking young people to design their own weather versions of feelings and discuss them in pairs. Try using photographs of people or emojis instead of weather. Ask the young people to notice when they 'meet these weather systems' over the course of a day or week. Talk to them about: how long the weather was with them, how it felt, how easy it was to notice and accept these different feelings.

2.9 Mindful Memories

Aims

- To use mindfulness to help regulate emotions based on our memories.

Resources

Script 6, 'Mindful Listening'; Worksheet 1, 'Mindful Breathing'.

Starter Activity

Introduce the activity: describe the way that we can use mindfulness to help us to regulate our emotions and let go when difficult thoughts or memories arise. We all have moments when past memories can feel upsetting or worrying. Feeling unhappy at times is normal for everyone. But it is not helpful or positive to have lots of negative memories and unhappy thoughts about ourselves. Through mindfulness we can notice and recognise these thoughts when we have them – when we do this we can then acknowledge them and let them go. We are going to do a listening meditation.

Main Activity

Script 6, 'Mindful Listening'.

End Activity

Worksheet 1, 'Mindful Breathing'.

Feedback

Talk to a partner about the sounds that you focused on – were they the same sounds?

Tips, Ideas & Extensions

Think about asking the young people to pay particular attention to the sounds surrounding them. Try a listening meditation practice at home.

2.10 'If' Questions

Aims

- To be mindful of possibilities.

Resources

Script 5, 'Full Body Scan'; Worksheet 16, '"If" Questions' (one for each person).

Starter Activity

Script 5, 'Full Body Scan'.

Main Activity

Explain the aim and session plan. Work through Worksheet 16, '"If" Questions', on your own.

End Activity

Compare your answers with a partner as appropriate.

Feedback

Talk to a partner about how you found today's session.

Tips, Ideas & Extensions

Ask young people to come up with some 'if' questions of their own and (as appropriate) interview each other. Ask them to speculate about, and discuss, how other people not in the room might answer, for example, friends, family, celebrities.

Looking for more ideas? Look at the 'Mindful Colouring' and 'Mazes' worksheets (Worksheets 4 & 5) and Worksheet 18, 'Visual Illusions'.

3

Working with Parents & Carers

Mindfulness is most effective when embedded into daily life, becoming a daily habit. Children and young people who are engaging in mindfulness practice are likely to benefit from complementary support at home. This requires their parents or carers to have knowledge and understanding of mindfulness, what their child is likely to be doing related to it, and how it might help their child.

You may wish to plan evenings or 'drop-in' sessions to support parents and carers in this area. Educational psychologists or other professionals may play a role here, or a member of school staff or a parent with interest and training in the area. Children and young people could also be involved in communicating their activities to parents and careers, for example, through a 'drop-in' or stall at an open, or parents', evening. Working together with young people on their 'Personal Mindfulness Record' (Resources Template 4) is another way that parents can be involved. It could be useful to provide a letter or leaflet for parents (see Resources Template 1, 'Information Sheet for Parents & Teachers') to support their understanding and involvement. Motivation may also be increased if the practice of mindfulness techniques is linked to relaxation and de-stressing, or if a parents' mindfulness group is set up.

The following activities may be an accessible and enjoyable way for parents and carers to join in or take away for home practice. You could produce an information booklet that includes a short introduction based on the templates in the Resources, as well as the following activities:

- Worksheet 17, '20 Ways to Reduce Stress during the Working Day'
- Activity 2.3,'Letter to Myself' from Section 2, 'Activities for Adolescents'

- Worksheet 2, 'Favourite Place'
- Worksheets 4, 5 & 18, 'Mindful Colouring', 'Mazes' and 'Visual Illusions'
- Worksheet 11, 'Relaxation Strategies'
- Script 6, 'Mindful Listening'

Working at Whole-School or Organisation Level

Just as children and young people seem to benefit most from mindfulness if their practice is 'joined up' to that of their parents or carers, implementing mindfulness as part of a whole-school or whole-organisation positive psychology approach is vital. As discussed in the Introduction, mindfulness should not be simply an extra-curricular activity or an add-on. Rather it works best if it forms part of the ethos of the entire school or organisation.

One element of working at this level is to provide those interacting with young people with the opportunity to develop their own practice, and to support them in doing so. This is likely to involve the provision of training and support, and the ring-fencing of specified times to carry out mindfulness activities. Ideally, appropriate rooms and time for carrying out the activities should be secured, and attendance at sessions should be voluntary. Staff members with an interest in mindfulness may wish to join in and support one another, but without organisational and emotional support from the broader school or organisation it may be difficult to maintain this interest.

Communication of exactly what mindfulness is and its links to whole-organisation ethos, policy and practice are important if staff are to support children and young people in their schools or groups and make informed decisions about their own mindfulness practice.

Some of the following sessions and activities may be useful within this context. The 'What is Mindfulness?' session is proposed an essential precursor to participation in the other activities.

'What is Mindfulness?' Session

An appropriately experienced or qualified person (for example, a mindfulness practitioner or an educational psychologist) could be asked to run this session. It might start by brainstorming ideas that people already have about mindfulness, including their concerns and confusions. These can be discussed in the group. A definition of mindfulness should be given ('paying attention, being in the moment, on purpose, non-judgementally') and discussed. Script 5, 'Full Body Scan', could be done now, followed by the introduction of the following activities, perhaps produced in booklet form.

- The table outlining the use of the Mindfulness Scripts (see Introduction) and the text of the scripts (Resources, Scripts 1–9)
- Worksheet 17, '20 Ways to Reduce Stress during the Working Day'
- Activity 2.3,'Letter to Myself' from Section 2, 'Activities for Adolescents'
- Worksheet 2, 'Favourite Place'
- Worksheets 4, 5 & 18, 'Mindful Colouring', 'Mazes' and 'Visual Illusions'
- Worksheet 11, 'Relaxation Strategies'
- Worksheet 7, 'Sounds of Nature'

5

Working with Children & Young People with Special Educational Needs (SEN)

When thinking about ways to use mindfulness with children and young people with special educational needs, there are a number of points to consider. First, it is vital to have an understanding of the child or young person – think about their individual profile and consider how they may engage in a mindfulness exercise. When thinking about a child's needs, you may think about their literacy needs, attention needs, sensory needs, level of self-awareness and communication. The 'Brief Screening Tool for Young Children' (Resources Template 5) is a useful and quick tool for you to see whether a child may be able to access mindfulness exercises.

Consider the child or young person's developmental stage, rather than their chronological age. The activities in Sections 1 and 2 of this book are divided into those suitable for younger children or for adolescents, however, it may be more appropriate for you to take an activity from the section for younger children, even if you are working with a teenager. Before using a 'main activity', you may want to use shorter, starter activities, to introduce the exercises and see how the child or young person responds.

Try reducing the language – these scripts are written so they can be adapted to make them most appropriate for each individual. You may find it helpful to look through the scripts in advance and reduce the level of language for children with difficulties with their comprehension and receptive language skills.

A number of the activities and exercises have a sensory focus and these can be a fun and engaging way to introduce mindfulness techniques.

A number of the scripts and exercises invite children and young people to notice their emotions and reflect upon them; be aware that this type of question can be more difficult for those with autism spectrum disorder and social communication difficulties. These young people may benefit from more explicit modelling and altering the script to reduce the number of questions of this type.

Bear in mind that if you are using mindfulness when supporting young people with SEN, this is an opportunity to share and communicate about mindfulness with others who work with the child, such as carers or teaching assistants. For example, if you are using mindfulness with a whole class or group of children, a teaching assistant may be able to support a smaller group or individuals in practising the exercises.

All children and young people will benefit from starting with shorter mindfulness exercises and then slowly building up to longer ones. This is something to be particularly aware of with children and young people with SEN; it is better to have a brief and successful exercise, than to attempt a longer one that the child is not able to sustain.

Resources

Templates

Worksheets

Mindfulness Scripts

TEMPLATE 1

Information Sheet for Parents & Carers

An introduction

Mindfulness is an approach that aims to further develop children's life skills by helping them to self-regulate and self-calm, pay attention to themselves and the world they live in, and to effectively reflect on their actions and relationships.

Mindfulness has been described as: 'The awareness that emerges through paying attention on purpose, through the present moment non-judgementally, to the unfolding of experience moment by moment' (Williams et al., 2007).

The key aims of mindfulness are to develop the following:

- **Attention** awareness of emotions, thoughts, feelings and greater concentration.
- **Balance** time for you, time for family and friends, time for school and studying.
- **Compassion** self-acceptance, being non-judgemental.

Who is this for?

This approach can be used by all adults and children to increase self-awareness and support us in managing daily life, as well as stressful events. Mindfulness can help to support the following:

- Attention
- Social relationships
- Anxiety
- Memory
- Self-management
- Self-understanding
- Relaxation

Outline of mindfulness in a group setting

Mindfulness can teach young people new skills that can be used every day, and which will also ensure that they develop skills and strategies for well-being in the future. Mindfulness is about learning to pay attention to each and every moment, being non-judgemental and accepting who you are.

The purpose of the group is to develop a practice of mindfulness, to better understand ourselves and to allow ourselves to have feelings, without allowing the feelings to control us and our actions. Mindfulness aims to help young people to relax, to remain calm, to offer themselves compassion and not to constantly compare themselves with others, as this is a certain source of unhappiness.

page 1 of 2

Information Sheet for Parents & Carers

We will play lots of games and activities to learn about ourselves and each other – for example, games to help young people become more aware of physical sensations, thoughts and feelings, to slow down, to focus on breathing, or simply to be able to accept a thought, then to let it go.

We may practise these activities every day. Sometimes these will last for 2–3 minutes and sometimes they may last for 10 minutes. Sometimes we will do a whole session of 40 minutes, which will include a range of activities and discussion tasks. What is important to remember is that the more we practise the better our skills become.

Reinforcing skills at home

The children and young people can therefore practise mindful activities in a range of contexts – including at home. For this purpose, they will be given a 'Mindfulness Record' on which they can record their own mindful practice and think about how effective it is in terms of maintaining overall well-being.

TEMPLATE 2

Information Sheet for Young People

MINDFULNESS GROUP

Dear ____

This term you are invited to join a 'Mindfulness Group'. This information sheet will answer some of the questions you might have.

What is Mindfulness?

'The awareness that emerges through paying attention on purpose through the present moment non-judgementally to the unfolding of experience moment by moment.' (Kabat-Zinn)

What will we do?

There will be _____ sessions, designed to help you learn mindfulness techniques and ideas.

You will learn in a small group of around _____ children and _____ adults. Each session will teach you new skills to use in school and out of school!

What will be expected of me?

You will be encouraged to listen and talk in group discussions.

You will be asked to try out strategies in each session and at home.

You will be expected to be respectful of others in the group.

I look forward to working with you!

Sample Consent Letter for Parents & Carers

MINDFULNESS GROUP

Dear ____

__________ School/Group is offering your child the opportunity to take part in a _____ week 'Mindfulness Group' starting __________. The group will be run by _____, along with a member of school staff. It will take place on __________ at __________.

The programme aims to help children and young people to learn mindfulness techniques and ideas to support their well-being, both within school and out of school.

Enclosed is an information sheet that will provide more details about the group. Please fill in and return the slip below to ______________________________ if you would like your child to take part, and please do get in touch if you would like more information.

Yours sincerely,

Consent and Permissions

I agree to let my child participate in the sessions.

I understand that I can withdraw my child from the session at any time and do not have to state a reason.

Signed ____ *(parent/carer)*

Print name ____

Date ____

If you have any concerns or queries about this programme or require any further information, please contact:

School information

TEMPLATE 4

Personal Mindfulness Record

Please try to practise the mindful activities we use in the group as often as you can. For example, spending a few minutes each day practising breathing exercises will help them to become part of your normal everyday routine!

Note down in the chart what activity you tried, when you tried it and how it felt, what thoughts or feelings you had – and perhaps you could also give it a score out of 5.

You can try these activities at both home and school and then feedback to your group leader.

TEMPLATE 4

Personal Mindfulness Record

Where?	Activity	Thoughts/Feelings	Score
			/5
			/5
			/5
			/5
			/5
			/5
			/5
			/5
			/5

TEMPLATE 5

Brief Screening Tool for Young Children

To be filled in by an adult who knows the child well.

Question	Yes	Maybe	No
Does the child understand basic one-part instructions?			
Can the child sustain attention for at least 1 minute on a directed task (e.g., listening to the teacher)?			
Do you think the child has some awareness (or could learn some awareness) of their breath and body?			
Can the child name any feelings?			

If the answers are 'Yes' or 'Maybe' for questions 1–3, the child is likely to be able to access some of these activities.

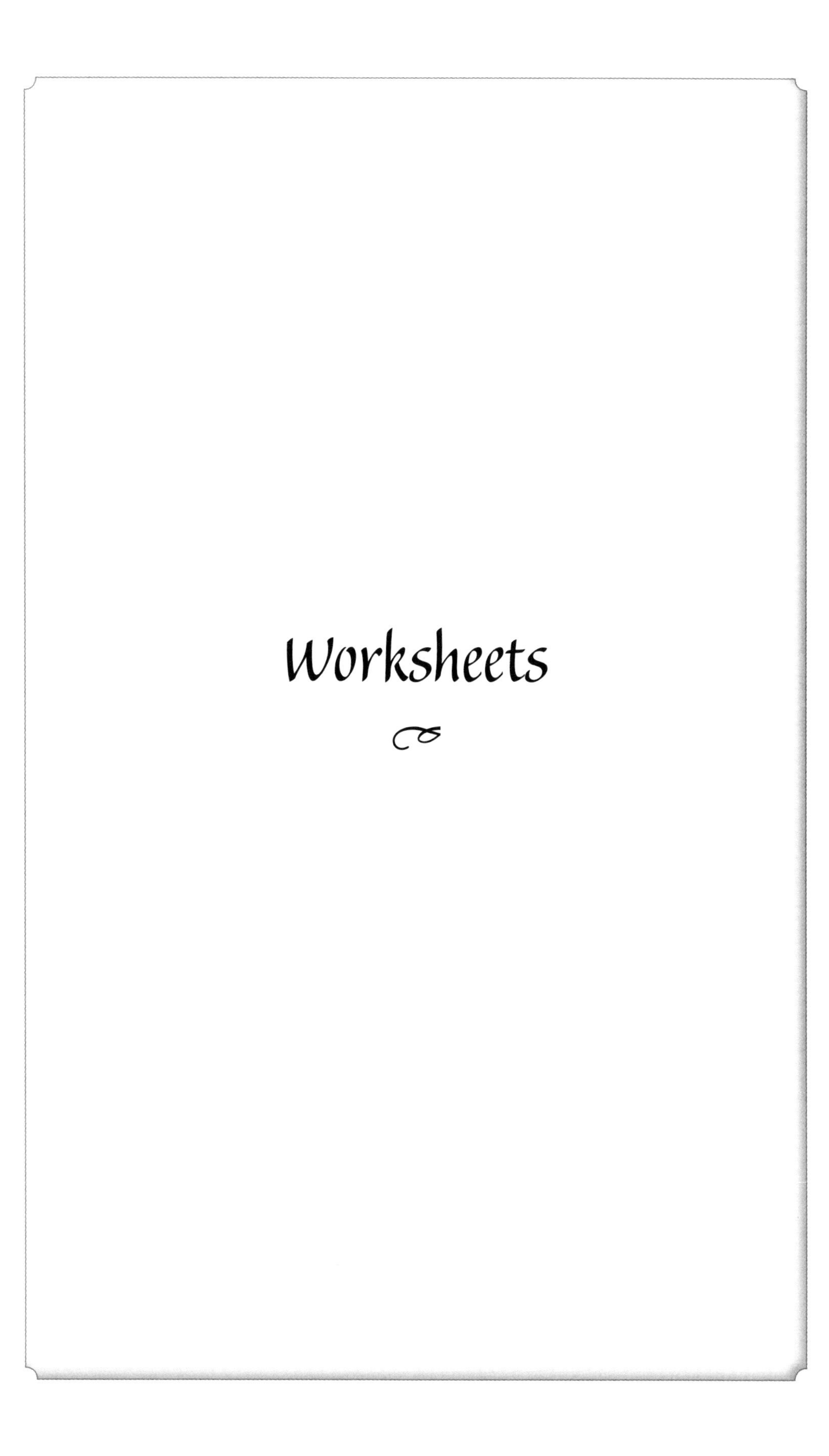

Worksheets

Mindful Breathing

Use these instructions to help you to relax and think about your breathing.

- Find a comfortable place to sit, with your eyes closed and your back reasonably straight.

- Focus your attention on your breathing.

- When a thought or feeling pops into your head, accept it, but allow it to float on by (imagine you are pinning your thoughts and feelings to a cloud,
or on a leaf floating down the river).

- Focus your attention on the rise and fall of your chest, the feeling of the air entering and leaving your body.

Activities: 1.1; 2.7

Worksheet 2 Favourite Place

- Try to create an image of your favourite or most special place.

- Think about somewhere that you would choose to go to relax.

- This place can be imaginary or real, inside or outside. Make sure you fill your special place with all the things you would like to help you relax.

- You could draw your favourite place, take a photograph and describe it, or make a collage from pictures in magazines and newspapers, as well as using crayons, paints and other materials to help make it come alive.

Activities: 1.2; 1.3; 1.4; 1.8; 1.9

Worksheet 3 Floating Balloons

Sit comfortably in your normal mindful breathing position (you could lie down flat on your back if it is more comfortable) and think about these words, while focusing on your breathing:

- Close your eyes and be very still.
- Imagine you are holding a big balloon.
- It is very light.
- This balloon is so light it starts to float up into the air.
- Hold on tight and feel the balloon gently rising into the sky.
- The big balloon is pulling you further and further into the air.
- Take a deep breath in and then breathe out slowly.
- Breathe in deeply, breathe out slowly.
- Each time you breathe in and out you gently glide further into the warm sky.
- Breathe in, breathe out. Breathe in, breathe out.
- Breathe in, breathe out. Breathe in, breathe out.

Using the hand you don't normally write with, try to draw and colour in a picture as well as you would if you were using your 'normal' or stronger hand.

While colouring, try to be mindful of how much concentration it is taking you! You may wish to think about what feelings you are experiencing in your arms and hands. Does it affect your shoulders, neck and head? What about the way you are sitting, and so on?

As an extension, you could try and write the alphabet, a sentence from a book, or your name!

Activities: 1.4; 2.10

Mazes

Spend some time focusing on one of the mazes, trying to complete it with as few errors as possible.

Try and be mindful of how you are processing along the routes, weaving through the maze in different directions.

If you want to make it more difficult, try completing the maze with your non-dominant hand (the one you don't normally write with)!

Activities: 1.4; 2.10

Worksheet 5 Mazes

Activities: 1.5; 2.2

WORKSHEET 6 Peaceful River

- Close your eyes, be very still, and imagine you are in a small boat.
- You are drifting down the river.
- Lie back and allow the soft breeze and river currents to move you gently along.
- As you lie there, let your whole body be completely still.
- You can feel the softness of the sunshine on your skin.
- You hear the birds singing quietly and the water rippling gently.
- You feel totally content and serene.
- As you lie there, let all the muscles in your body relax.
- Breathe in and out and feel yourself sinking deeper and deeper into relaxation.

Go outside and listen to the surrounding sounds for one minute, writing down all the different sounds you can hear on a blank piece of paper.

- To start with, you might find it useful to get comfy, sitting down, with your eyes closed.

- Try listening in different locations, at different times of the day.

- You may like to record the sounds you hear or just enjoy the time relaxing and tuning into your surroundings.

- Things you might hear during this activity: people; animals; transport; birds; and the weather.

Activities: 1.7; 1.10

WORKSHEET 8 Soaking Up Sunshine

Close your eyes, be very still and imagine you are lying down outside in the sunshine.

Your body feels totally relaxed.

As you lie comfortably in the soft grass:

- The rays of the sun are soaking into your muscles, warming and relaxing your whole body.
- Feel the warmth of the sun on your legs and let them relax.
- Let the muscles around your tummy relax.
- Feel the sun's rays on your shoulders and arms as you relax into the spongy grass.
- Now feel the warm sun on your face.
- As the sun touches your whole face it relaxes.
- Relax your forehead, your cheeks, your eyes and your mouth.

Relax ...

Activities: 1.8; 2.4

Worksheet 9 Cards for Relaxation Zones

Zone One: Music

- Sit or lie comfortably.
- Close your eyes if you are happy to do so.
- Listen to your breath and relax.
- When you feel ready, put on the headphones and listen to the music.
- Really attend to the music.
- If thoughts come into your head, notice them and let them go.

Try the other types of music and think about what you found most relaxing.

Zone Two: Soft Area

- Sit or lie comfortably.
- Close your eyes if you are happy to do so.
- Listen to your breath and relax.
- Notice how you feel.
- Really attend to how your body feels: your feet, your legs, your shoulders, your hands ...
- If thoughts come into your head, notice them and let them go.

Try out different areas in this zone and think about where was most relaxing for you.

Zone Three: Lights

- Sit or lie comfortably.
- Attend to the area around you.
- Notice the things you can see around you.
- Listen to your breath and relax.
- If thoughts come into your head, notice them and let them go.
- Close your eyes slightly if you are happy to and notice the light around you.

Think about how relaxing you found this area.

Activities: 1.8; 2.4

WORKSHEET 10 Personal Relaxation Grid

Relaxation	Rating 0–10 *(10 is the best and 0 is the worst)*	Comments
Relaxation Areas		
Light Area		
Soft Area		
Music Area		
Relaxation Strategies		
Lemon		
Mud		
Stretch		
Wrinkle		
Shrug		
Jaw clench		

Activities: 1.8; 2.4

WORKSHEET 11 Relaxation Strategies

Here are some relaxation strategies for you to try:

- Squeeze a lemon in your hands, releasing the lemon juice into a bowl.
- Stretch your arms over your head, reaching for the sky.
- Shrug your shoulders tight and curl up into a ball, as if you were hiding in a tortoise's shell.
- Wrinkle your nose as if you are trying to get a bug off your nose.
- Clench your jaw really tight – and then release.
- Imagine it has been raining and you are standing barefoot in mud! Imagine that you are squishing your toes in the mud – wriggle your toes about in your shoes.

Activity: 1.9

WORKSHEET 12 Bears with Feelings

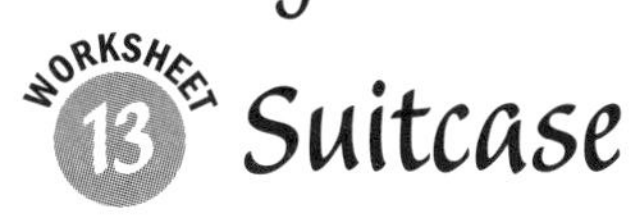

Activity: 2.5 Worksheet 13 Suitcase

Imagine you are given a suitcase in which to pack all the important aspects of your life right now.

- Spend some time being mindful of all the people, places, things, values and other things that you consider the most important.
- Draw, write or add pictures of all of your choices, so that they circle the suitcase.

Activity: 2.6

WORKSHEET 14 Pleasant Events

Be aware of one pleasant event or occurrence each day *while* it is happening. Record your experience below.

	What was the experience?	Were you aware of the pleasant feelings while the event was happening?	How did your body feel, in detail, during this experience?	What moods, feelings, and thoughts accompanied this event?	What thoughts are in your mind right now, as you write this down?
Monday					
Tuesday					
Wednesday					
Thursday					
Friday					
Saturday					
Sunday					

Activity: 2.8

WORKSHEET 15 Weather Pictures

Activity: 2.8

WORKSHEET 15

Weather Pictures

'If' Questions

Think about the possibilities when you are asked some 'what if?' questions.

- If you had a million pounds, what would you do?
- If you could have a super power, what would it be and why?
- If you could be an animal, which one would you choose and why?
- If you could visit anywhere on the planet, where would you choose and why?
- If you ruled the world for a day, what changes would you make and why?

Can you create any of your own?

20 Ways to Reduce Stress during the Working Day

1 Take a few minutes in the morning to be quiet and meditate – sit or lie down and 'be' with yourself ... gazing out of the window, listening to the sounds of nature, or taking a slow, quiet walk.

2 While your car is warming up, take a minute to quietly pay attention to your breathing.

3 While driving, become aware of body tension, for example, hands wrapped tightly around the steering wheel, shoulders raised, stomach tight, and so on. Consciously work at releasing, dissolving that tension. Does being tense help you to drive better? What does it feel like to relax and drive?

4 Decide not to play the radio and just 'be' with yourself.

5 Stay in the correct lane and drive at 55 miles per hour.

6 Pay attention to your breathing or to the sky, trees, and so on, when stopped at a red light.

7 After parking your car, take a moment to orient yourself to your working day.

8 While sitting at your desk, keyboard, or other work position, monitor your bodily sensations and tension levels, and consciously attempt to relax and let go of excess tension.

9 Use your breaks to truly relax, rather than simply 'pause'. For example, instead of having coffee or a cigarette, take a 2- to 5-minute walk, or sit at your desk and recoup.

10 At lunch, changing your environment can be helpful. You could even just try closing the door (if you have one) and take some time to consciously relax.

11 Decide to 'stop' for 1 to 3 minutes every hour during the working day. Become aware of your breathing and bodily sensations. Use it as a time to regroup and recoup.

12 Use the everyday cues in your environment as reminders to 'centre' yourself, for example, when the telephone is ringing, while turning on the computer, and so on.

13 Take some time at lunch or break to share with close colleagues. Choose topics not necessarily work-related.

page 1 of 2

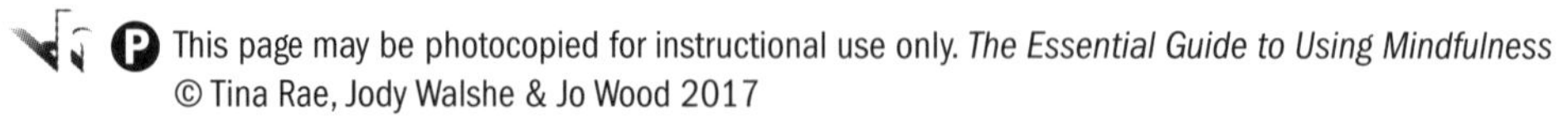

20 Ways to Reduce Stress during the Working Day

14 Choose to eat one or two lunches per week in silence. Use it as a time to eat slowly and 'be' with yourself.

15 At the end of the day, retrace your activities of the day, acknowledging and congratulating yourself on what you've accomplished and make a list of activities for tomorrow.

16 Pay attention to the short walk to your car, consciously breathing. Notice the feelings in your body, try to accept them rather than resist them. Listen to the sounds outside the office. Can you walk without feeling rushed?

17 While your car is warming up, sit quietly, and consciously make the transition from work to home. Take a moment to simply 'be'; enjoy it for a moment. Like most of us, you're heading into your next full-time job: home.

18 While driving, notice if you're rushing. What does this feel like? What could you do about it? Remember, you've got more control than you imagine.

19 When you pull into the drive or park your car, take a minute to come back to the present. Orient yourself to being with your family or household members.

20 Change out of work clothes when you get home; it helps you to make a smoother transition into your next 'role'. You can spare the 5 minutes to do this. Say hello to each of the family members; centre yourself at home. If possible, make the time to take 5 to 10 minutes to be quiet and still.

Activity: 2.10

WORKSHEET 18 Visual Illusions

Take a look at the following images and locate the optical illusions (the pictures that come out of the photos).

Different people may interpret the same picture in different ways. The same can be said about everyday encounters and situations.

Whilst looking at the illusions, think about some everyday scenarios that could be perceived differently by other people and how some of the things you feel and observe could be thought of in a different way.

Mindfulness Scripts

Activities: 1.3; 3.1

SCRIPT 1

Mini Script

- Close your eyes and focus your attention on your breath.
- Now send all your attention to your hand.
- Be aware of how your hand feels as it picks up an object.
- Be aware of how you feel about picking up this object.
- Feel the object in your hand. Feeling the object ... touching the object ...
- Send all your awareness to this object. Is it heavy? Soft? Cold? Sticky?
- Now move your attention away from your hand and back to the sounds of the room around you.
- Open your eyes.

SCRIPT 2 Introduction to Meditation

This is a good introductory meditation as it begins to raise sensory awareness very simply – by focusing on the breath. The breath is a useful focus, because it reminds us that we are in the present ('this is what is happening now') and because it connects us to our senses and how we feel.

This is a 1-minute meditation. Slowly start to relax. I will talk you through it step-by-step and tell you when to stop. You can close your eyes if you like, or try looking down or focusing gently on something in the distance.

Sit up straight, but relaxed. Take your back away from your chair so that you are not using it for support. Your feet should be flat on the floor, with your hands resting gently on your thighs. PAUSE.

Now, begin to focus your attention on your breath as it flows in and out of your body. Breathe naturally and notice each breath. In ... out ... Tune in to your natural breathing pattern. In ... out ...

Don't worry if your mind starts to wander, or thoughts pop in. Notice these thoughts, but always refocus your attention on your breath. PAUSE. Keep listening to your breath. In ... out ... It's fine to notice your thoughts.

page 1 of 2

SCRIPT 2 Introduction to Meditation

It's fine to be interested in your thoughts. Don't try to ignore them, just accept them and think back to your breath. Listen to your breath. Try to notice your thoughts without judging them or thinking too much about them. Bring your attention back to your breath. PAUSE.

That is the end of the minute. When you feel ready, open your eyes and bring your attention back to the room. Don't rush. Just slowly bring your attention back.

Activity: 1.6 Script 3 Mindful Mouth

This script draws awareness to our sense of taste and smell. When we eat, we often do so without really focusing on the taste, smell or texture of the food.

For this activity it is suggested you use a tasty item of food, such as a cherry tomato, a chocolate raisin, a grape, a piece of chocolate, a Malteser ...

We start by taking your attention to the piece of food you have selected to eat. Look very closely at it, as if this were the first time you have seen it before. Begin to notice how it feels in your hand PAUSE. The texture of it in contact with your fingers. Look carefully: what do you notice about the colours?

Notice and recognise any thoughts that you may be having about this food. Be aware of any feelings you may be having as you look at the food.

Now, in your own time, begin to move the food up to your nose. Smell it. PAUSE. What do you notice? Once you have smelt it, take it to your mouth. PAUSE. As you are moving it towards to your mouth, be aware of your arm and hand moving ... PAUSE.

Activity: 1.6

Mindful Mouth

If your mind wanders ... gently and non-judgementally bring it back.

Slowly put the food into your mouth. Notice the taste, the texture and the sensation. Attend to these sensations; really notice the qualities of the food as you hold it in your mouth. PAUSE.

Bring your attention to the sensations as you hold it in your mouth. PAUSE.

When you feel ready to swallow, notice the feeling and experience it with awareness. Once you have eaten the food take, your attention to the sensations and tastes left in your mouth.

Finally, attend to any thoughts you noticed as you reflect on the experience.

SCRIPT 4

Progressive Muscle Relaxation

This works on drawing awareness to the present experience of the body and the way that we can learn to consciously 'scan' it and relax it, part by part. It is good to relieve tension and worry.

We will be performing an exercise to help you relax your body and mind. You will be asked to tense and relax different muscles around your body. If you feel any pain or discomfort in any particular muscle, just skip that step.

Find a comfortable position that you think you can maintain for the duration of this exercise. You may close your eyes or, if you prefer to keep your eyes open, try to focus on a particular spot.

Focus on your body. Don't worry if you notice your mind starting to wander, just bring your attention back to the muscle we are working on. Take a deep breath in, hold it briefly, and exhale slowly. Repeat this a few times and notice air entering and leaving your lungs.

Wrinkle up your forehead and notice where it feels most tense. Hold for 5 seconds, and release. Notice how it feels to loosen your muscles.

Close your eyes very tight. Hold for 5 seconds, and release.

page 1 of 2

SCRIPT 4 Progressive Muscle Relaxation

Tighten the back of your neck by gently pulling your head backwards with your hands. Hold for 5 seconds, and release.

Straighten your right arm, tighten your triceps, and clench your right fist. Hold for 5 seconds, and release. Repeat with your left arm.

Flex your right arm and tighten your biceps. Hold for 5 seconds, and release. Repeat with your left arm.

Lift your shoulders up and try to reach for your ears. Hold for 5 seconds, and release.

Pull your shoulders back and tighten your upper back. Hold for 5 seconds, and release.

Tighten your chest. Hold for 5 seconds, and release. Tighten your stomach muscles/abdominals. Hold for 5 seconds, and release.

Lift your right leg, pull your toes inward. Hold for 5 seconds, and release. Repeat with your left leg.

Tighten your thighs. Hold for 5 seconds, and release.

Gradually relax your whole body. Imagine a wave of relaxation moving through your whole body, from your head, down to your toes. Take a deep breath in, and out ...

Activities: 2.1; 2.3; 2.5; 2.7; 2.8; 2.10

SCRIPT 5 Full Body Scan

This script raises sensory and bodily awareness.

Short or introductory version

Start by focusing on the breath. Feel your breath entering and leaving your body. Notice how it feels. Really focus on this feeling. If thoughts pop into your head or your mind wanders, notice this and refocus on your breathing. Notice the in-breath and the out-breath. In ... out ...

Next take your full attention to your feet. Feel their contact with the ground.

Next take your full attention to the backs of your legs ...

Next move all your attention slowly up your spine. Try to sense each vertebra ... move up the back to the shoulder blades. PAUSE. Think about how they feel right now ... tight? ... relaxed?

Next bring all your attention to your face. Bring your attention back to the here and now and your breath if your mind wanders. PAUSE. When you are ready, slowly open your eyes ...

Activities: 2.1; 2.3; 2.5; 2.7; 2.8; 2.10

SCRIPT 5 Full Body Scan

Longer version

Start by focusing on the breath. Feel your breath entering and leaving your body. Notice how it feels. Really focus on this feeling. If thoughts pop into your head or your mind wanders, notice this without judgement and refocus on your breathing. Notice the in-breath and the out-breath. In ... out ...

Next take your full attention to the soles of your feet. Feel their contact with the ground. Can you feel the contact between the bottom of your feet and your shoes? PAUSE. Feel for tightness, heat, cold, movement. Concentrate fully on your feet ... now ... in the present moment. It is likely that your mind will wander off to other places, but keep bringing it back to your feet ... the soles of your feet. PAUSE. Notice the thoughts that flit in and then bring your attention back to your feet. PAUSE.

Next take your full attention to the backs of your legs ... your ankles ... your calves ... the back of each knee in turn ... the back of your heels. Maybe you have never attended to the back of your heels before. Really attend to how they feel. PAUSE.

SCRIPT 5

Full Body Scan

Now bring your full attention to the front of your knees. Are they touching your clothing or are they exposed to the air? Or are they touching the table? PAUSE.

Consciously explore your contact with your chair. Think about how this feels. If thoughts come into your head, gently notice them and push them away.

Next move all your attention slowly up your spine. Try to sense each vertebra ... Can you feel your vertebrae? If you cannot, acknowledge this without judgement and steadily return your attention to your back. Move up the back to the shoulder blades. PAUSE. Think about how they feel right now ... tight? ... relaxed? ... warm? PAUSE. Think about how they feel to you right now.

Now move your full attention round to the front. Notice your stomach and chest. Can you feel any movement in the stomach? Can you feel any tightness in your chest?

Next bring all your attention to your face. Think about how it feels. Any tension? ...hot? ... cold? Attend to your nose ... eyes ... lips... cheeks ... forehead ... ears... PAUSE. Bring your attention back to the here and now and your bodily experiences if your mind wanders. PAUSE. When you are ready, slowly open your eyes ...

Activity: 2.9

SCRIPT 6 Mindful Listening

This script works on placing focus on the present to regulate emotions. It helps us to recognise our memories, but not to feel tied to them.

We are going to recognise memories and negative thoughts as we have them. We notice these thoughts and become aware that we do not need to hold onto these thoughts. They are simply thoughts. We can notice them and let them go. By focusing our attention on bodily sensations, such as our hearing, we can develop our ability to let go of these memories and thoughts. We can learn to focus our sense of hearing and use this to practise letting go of memories or negative thoughts coming into our mind. We are going to do a 'listening meditation'.

Sit in or on a chair. Sit up straight. You can close your eyes, or focus your gaze on the floor in front of you. PAUSE.

Begin by focusing your attention on the sounds around you ... take a couple of minutes to notice the different sounds around you. You are sitting in the present moment. PAUSE. Become more and more aware of the sounds you are hearing. If you notice your mind

page 1 of 2

Activity: 2.9

Mindful Listening

begin to wander and you become aware of thoughts, acknowledge those thoughts and then gently bring your attention back to the sounds you can hear.

Really use your hearing. Start to try to focus on particular sounds ... what qualities do these sounds have? Gentle? Fast? Comforting? Heavy?

Now try to focus on the sounds themselves, rather than the object making the sounds.

Are you noticing any thoughts? Let them go and gently bring your focus back to the sounds you are hearing. PAUSE.

To conclude, move your attention to focus on any sounds you can hear in your body. Can you hear your breath? Your heart beating? Buzzing, or other sounds in your ears? PAUSE. Now finish by bringing your attention back to your breathing. What sounds do you notice when you breathe?

Now ... when you feel ready ... open your eyes.

SCRIPT 7

Mindful Looking

This script draws awareness to the present, using nature. Considerable evidence indicates that feeling aware of and connected to nature has a positive impact on our well-being. Appreciating nature can also help us to put our thoughts into perspective. This script helps to focus on the breathing, the body and nature; grounding ourselves in the present and not worrying too much about the future.

To start with find a comfortable place to sit, where you can look out at some natural surroundings. If you cannot access such a view, you may wish to focus on a vase of flowers or indoor plant.

We will start by gently taking our attention to our bodily sensations. Sit up, with a good posture that you can sustain. Start by looking out of the window and taking your full awareness to your feet. The soles of your feet ... PAUSE. Notice the feeling of your feet in the shoes you have on, or the points of contact where your feet are touching the ground. Are you noticing any tension? Warmth? Coolness? Really notice your feet right now, in the present moment.

SCRIPT 7

Mindful Looking

If you feel your mind begin to wander, quietly observe this, acknowledge it, and then gently bring your attention back to the sensations in your feet. It is normal for the mind to wander, so just bring your focus gently back to your point of attention, your feet. PAUSE. Each time you notice your mind wandering, observe this, acknowledge this, and then bring your attention back to your feet. Be aware of your feet as you sit looking out of the window.

We are now going to focus our attention on the natural environment. Take notice of the space you are looking at. Is it a large open area, or is it quite small? Notice how you respond to this. PAUSE.

Draw your attention to exploring distance and space – can you see the furthest point in the distance? Explore the horizon. PAUSE. Are there more enclosed areas with trees, hedges, bushes? Are there open spaces? PAUSE. Observe when your attention wanders. Gently accept this. Notice it. Bring your focus back. You are aware that you are curious about where your thoughts have wandered, but you can let these thoughts go ...

SCRIPT 7

Mindful Looking

Begin now to focus on the sounds around you. Can you notice any natural sounds? Can you hear the weather? Birds? Rustling leaves? Separate the qualities of these sounds from the objects making the sounds. What qualities do the sounds have? Light? Heavy? Soothing? Really focus on the qualities of these sounds. How are you responding to the qualities of these sounds? Notice the effect these sounds have for you ... non-judgementally ... PAUSE.

You have been aware of the sounds around you, and now you are taking your focus to what you can see. Really take your attention to what you can see. PAUSE. You may want to focus on something particular and notice the colour, texture, shade, light. Explore what you can see.

As you look outside can you see movement? Stillness? Explore the movements you see. Focus your attention on the movement ... it might be the waving of leaves on trees, or the flight of birds. Carefully and non-judgementally consider the movements you can see. PAUSE.

SCRIPT 7

Mindful Looking

Now turn your attention to what is still in the natural environment you are looking at. Where is the stillness as you look outside? What do you notice about the stillness? Is it calm? Restful? As you notice these qualities, non-judgementally, be aware of the effect on you. PAUSE.

We are now going to finish by returning from looking outside back to exploring the sensations of your whole body. Focus on how you are feeling in the present moment. Let go of thoughts of the past or the future. The experience of 'now'. As we finish, reflect on how you found this.

SCRIPT 8 Mindful Movement

This will involve focusing mindfully our body's movements. We hold a stress within our body and movement can lift mood and relieve stress. This also helps to turn our attention to being grateful for our bodies and what they can do.

Start by standing up. Straighten your back. Be aware of how your body feels as you stand straight. PAUSE. Now begin to take your focus down to the soles of your feet. What do you notice? What sensations are you aware of as your feet are in contact with the ground? What does the ground feel like? Do you notice stability? Roughness? Other textures? As you focus on yourself standing on the ground ... notice ... has your mind wandered? If it has wandered, gently bring it back to the soles of your feet and you stand tall.

Now stretch and reach your arms upwards ... notice the different bodily sensations as you do. Now, slowly and carefully bringing your arms back towards your sides, letting your hands hang ... PAUSE.

Now begin to walk carefully, slowly, gently around the space. You walk very often but, as you walk now, you are aware of the sensations in your feet. Take your attention to your feet as they step ... PAUSE. Which part of your

SCRIPT 8

Mindful Movement

foot touches the ground first as you take a step? What happens to your foot as you step on the ground and then lift it? PAUSE.

It is normal for your mind to wander. If you notice this, just gently bring your focus back to your feet as you are walking. PAUSE.

As you keep walking, move your attention from your feet to exploring the sensations in your legs. Notice your knees as you walk. Do they feel tense? Relaxed? What do you notice as you take each step? Take your attention to the shifting of your weight with each step. PAUSE. Really notice the sensations. PAUSE.

Now begin to move your attention to your back and spine. PAUSE. Without judgement, notice how your back and spine feel ... explore the sensations ... is there tension? What do you notice? If you feel your mind wandering, gently bring it back to your spine. PAUSE.

Now take your attention to your whole body at the same time. In the moment. As you walk. Take each careful step and sense your body as a whole. PAUSE. Notice your breathing and how this impacts your whole body. PAUSE.

SCRIPT 8 Mindful Movement

When you are ready, begin to slow down and stop. Stand still, straight and tall. PAUSE. You may want to look at the ground or close your eyes. PAUSE. As you stand still, notice the sense of your whole body. When you are ready, open your eyes or look up.

SCRIPT 9

Kindness & Gratitude

Start by focusing on the breath. Feel your breath entering and leaving your body. Notice how it feels. Really focus on this feeling. If thoughts pop into your head or your mind wanders, notice this and refocus on your breathing. Notice the in breath and the out breath. In ... out ...

Next take your full attention to your feet. Feel their contact with the ground.

Next take your full attention to the backs of your legs ...

Next move all your attention slowly up your spine. Try to sense each vertebra. Move up the back to the shoulder blades. PAUSE. Think about how they feel right now ... tight? ... relaxed? ...

Next bring all your attention to your face. Bring your attention back to the here and now and your breath if your mind wanders. PAUSE.

Now start to think about a person you love ... really think about them and bring them to mind ... look at their face in your mind and explore their features ... think about how you feel about them ... notice how you feel and how your body feels ...how your breath feels ... notice your breath ...

SCRIPT 9 Kindness & Gratitude

Think about this person that you love and recognise that they want, or have wanted, to be happy and at peace. Say to yourself, 'May (s)he be happy and healthy and at peace' ... PAUSE. Listen ... notice your body and your breathing ...

Now start to think about a person you find difficult or have found difficult in the past. This might be someone that you would like to make peace with and forgive ... explore their face and features in your mind ... see them... PAUSE. Explore their features and qualities without judgement.

Now start to notice any reactions in your body ... PAUSE. Think about this person without judgement, accept them as they are ... Recognise that they want, or have wanted, to be happy and at peace.

Hold them in your mind. Say to yourself, 'May (s)he be happy and healthy and at peace' ... PAUSE. Listen ... notice your body and your breathing ...

Notice the sensations in your body, whilst you are saying to yourself, 'May (s)he be happy and healthy and at peace' ... Explore whether it is possible to examine these feelings without holding back your feelings and without

SCRIPT 9

Kindness & Gratitude

judging yourself. If at any time you feel overwhelmed, draw your attention back to your breath ... in the present moment ... Treat yourself kindly ... Accept yourself ...

Now slowly open your eyes and think about how you found this exercise. Talk to someone about it if you would like to.

References

Baer R.A., 2003, 'Mindfulness Training as a Clinical Intervention: A Conceptual and Empirical Review', *Clinical Psychology: Science and Practice* 10, pp125–43.

Benn R., Akiva T., Arel S. & Roeser R.W., 2012, 'Mindfulness Training Effects for Parents and Educators of Children with Special Needs', *Developmental Psychology* 48 (5), pp1476–87.

Burke C.A., 2010, 'Mindfulness-Based Approaches with Children and Adolescents: A Preliminary Review of Current Research in an Emergent Field', *Journal of Child and Family Studies* 19, pp133–44.

Ciarrochi J., Kashdan T.B. & Harris R., 2013, 'The Foundations of Flourishing', Kashdan T.B. & Ciarrochi J. (eds), *Mindfulness, Acceptance, and Positive Psychology: The Seven Foundations of Well-Being*, Context Press, Oakland.

Craig C., 2007, *Creating Confidence: A Handbook for Professionals Working with Young People*, The Centre for Confidence and Wellbeing, Glasgow.

Csíkszentmihályi M., 1991, *Flow: The Psychology of Optimal Experience*, Harper & Row, New York.

Davidson R.J. & Lutz A., 2008, 'Buddha's Brain: Neuroplasticity and Meditation [In the Spotlight', *IEEE Signal Processing Magazine* 25 (1), pp176–174.

Davidson R.J., Kabat-Zinn J., Schumacher J., Rosenkranz M., Muller D., Santorelli S.F., Urbanowski F., Harrington A., Bonus K. & Sheridan J.F., 2003, 'Alterations in Brain and Immune Function Produced by Mindfulness Meditation', *Psychosomatic Medicine* 65, pp564–70.

Davis T.J., 2012, 'Mindfulness-Based Approaches and their Potential for Educational Psychology Practice', *Educational Psychology in Practice* 28 (1), pp31–46.

Eysenck M. & Keane M.T., 2010, *Cognitive Psychology*, Psychology Press, Hove.

Franco C., Mañas I., Cangas A., Moreno E. & Gallego J., 2010, 'Reducing Teachers' Psychological Distress through Mindfulness Training', *Spanish Journal of Psychology* 13 (2), pp655–66.

Fredrickson B., 2009, *Positivity – Groundbreaking Research to Release Your Inner Optimist and Thrive*, One World, Oxford.

Germer C.K., 2005, 'Mindfulness: What is It? What does It Matter?', Germer C.K., Siegel R.D. & Fulton P.R. (eds), *Mindfulness and Psychotherapy* , Guilford Press, New York.

Gold E., Smith A., Hopper I., Herne D., Tansey G. & Hulland C., 2010, 'Mindfulness-Based Stress Reduction (MBSR) for Primary School Teachers', *Journal of Child and Family Studies* 19 (2), pp184–9.

Greeson J.M., 2009, 'Mindfulness Research Update 2008', *Complimentary Health Practice Review* 14 (1), pp10–18.

Grenville-Cleave B., 2012, *Introducing Positive Psychology: A Practical Guide*, Icon Books, London.

Harnett P.S. & Dawe S., 2012, 'Review: The Contribution of Mindfulness-Based Therapies for Children and Families and Proposed Conceptual Integration', *Child and Adolescent Mental Health* 17 (4), pp195–208.

Hofmann S.G., Sawyer A.T., Witt A.A. & Oh D., 2010, 'The Effect of Mindfulness-Based Therapy on Anxiety and Depression: A Meta-Analytic Review', *Journal of Consulting and Clinical Psychology* 78 (2), pp169–83.

Huppert F.A. & Johnson D.M., 2010, 'A Controlled Trial of Mindfulness Training Schools: The Importance of Practice for an Impact on Wellbeing', *The Journal of Positive Psychology* 5 (4), pp264–74.

James W., 2008, *The Principles of Psychology*, Volume 1, Dover Books: New York.

Joyce A., Etty-Leal J., Zazryn T., Hamilton A. & Hassed C., 2010, 'Exploring a Mindfulness Meditation Program on the Mental Health of Upper Primary Children: A Pilot Study', *Advances in School Mental Health Promotion* 3, p.17.

Kostanski M. & Hassed C., 2008, 'Mindfulness as a Concept and a Process', *Australian Psychologist* 43, pp15–21.

Kuyken W., Weare K., Ukoumunne O.C., Vicary R., Motton N., Burnett R., Cullen C., Hennelly S. & Huppert F., 2013, 'Effectiveness of the Mindfulness in Schools Programme: Non-Randomised Controlled Feasibility Study', *British Journal of Psychiatry* 203 (2), pp126–31.

Manas I.M., Justo C.F. & Martinez E.J., 2011, 'Reducing Levels of Teacher Stress and the Days of Sick Leave in Secondary School Teachers through a Mindfulness Training Program', *Clinicia Y Salud* 22 (2), pp121–37.

Napoli M., Krech P.R. & Holley L.C., 2005, 'Mindfulness Training for Elementary School Students: The Attention Academy', *Journal of Applied School Psychology* 21,pp 99–125.

National Institute of Clinical Excellence, 2009, 'Depression: The Treatment and Management of Depression in Adults, http://www.nice.org.uk/nicemedia/pdf/CG90NICEguideline.pdf

Rasmussen M.K. & Pidgeon A.M., 2011, 'The Direct and Indirect Benefits of Dispositional Mindfulness on Self-Esteem and Social Anxiety', *Anxiety, Stress, & Coping* 24 (2), pp227–33.

Schonert-Reichl K.A. & Lawlor M.S., 2010, 'The Effects of a Mindfulness-Based Education Program on Pre- and Early Adolescents' Well-Being and Social and Emotional Competence', *Mindfulness* 1, pp137–51.

Seligman M.E.P., 2002, *Authentic Happiness*, Free Press, New York.

Semple R.J. & Burke C.A., 2011, 'Treating Children and Adolescents with Mindfulness', Kendall P.C. (ed.), *Child and Adolescent Therapy: Cognitive-Behavioural Procedures*, 4th edn, Guilford Press, New York.

Semple R.J., Reid E.F.G. & Miller L., 2005, 'Treating Anxiety with Mindfulness: An Open Trial of Mindfulness Training for Anxious Children', *Journal of Cognitive Psychotherapy* 19, pp379–92.

Vickery C.E. & Dorjee D., 2016, 'Mindfulness Training in Primary Schools Decreases Negative Affect and Increases Meta-Cognition in Children', *Frontiers in Psychology* 6(2025), Published online doi: 10.3389/fpsyg.2015.02025.

Virgili M., 2013, 'Mindfulness-Based Interventions Reduce Psychological Distress in Working Adults: A Meta-Analysis of Intervention Studies', *Mindfulness*, Published online doi: 10.1007/s12671-013-0264-0.

Weare K., 2013, 'Developing Mindfulness with Children and Young People: A Review of the Evidence and Policy Context', *Journal of Children's Services* 8, Published online doi: 10.1108/JCS-12-2012-0014.

Weare K., 2012, 'Evidence for the Impact of Mindfulness on Children and Young People. The Mindfulness in School Project.' Retrieved on 02/12/13 from http://www.enhancementthemes.ac.uk/docs/documents/impact-of-mindfulness--katherine-weare.pdf

Williams M., Segal Z., Teasdale J. & Kabat-Zinn J., 2007, *The Mindful Way through Depression Freeing Yourself from Chronic Unhappiness*, Guildford Press: New York.

Williams M. & Penman D., 2011, *Mindfulness: A Practical Guide to Finding Peace in a Frantic World*, Piatkus, London.

The Essential Guides

All ages

Practical and user-friendly introductions that will enable professionals to use tried-and-tested strategies and techniques when working with young people to promote emotional and mental well-being.

These useful tools will help to prevent the escalation of difficulties and will provide anyone wishing to develop a programme of support with a range of problem-solving ideas and techniques.

The Essential Guide to using Mindfulness with Children & Young eople

Tina Rae, Jody Walshe & Jo Wood

A practical, user-friendly introduction to key tools and strategies.

Mindfulness can help young people to develop the ability to calm themselves; to pay attention to themselves in the world and to think about and reflect upon their actions and relationships.

These practical skills can help build resilience and manage anxiety and stress through increased sensory awareness; regulation of emotions and attention and acceptance of thoughts and feelings.

Through these easy to use techniques, young people will be better able to manage social relationships, anxiety levels, memory, self-understanding and relaxation.

The Essential Guide to Solution Focused Brief Therapy (SBFT) with Children & Young People

Tina Rae & Miles Thomas

Help young people to learn to devise solutions and to focus on the future rather than the past.

Solution focused brief therapy is based on solution-building rather than problem solving. It encourages people to explore their current resources and future hopes rather than focusing upon present problems and their past causes.

Outlines key techniques and strategies that have been shown to be effective across a wide range of difficulties and problems, however serious these may seem.

Explains clearly how and why to use these successful methods to help young people find solutions, build confidence and reach their goals.

The Essential Guide to Cognitive Behaviour Therapy (CBT) with Children & Young People

Tina Rae & Pandora Giles

Learn how to use this effective problem-solving technique to help young people.

CBT is an effective intervention for anyone helping young people with emotional problems and difficulties. It emphasises the role that thoughts play in both emotions and behaviours and focuses on the fact that changing thought processes can have a significant effect on altering behaviours. It can result in positive changes over a short period of time.

Through the use of problem-solving skills young people can learn to reconsider negative assumptions and reframe their self-perception to improve their emotional well-being.

Full of easy-to-use practical techniques and strategies.

The Essential Guide to Positive Psychology with Children & Young People

Tina Rae & Helena Bunn

Help young people to recognise their strengths and use these to build confidence for the future.

Emotional well-being is not a stand-alone feature but is linked to our ability to flourish and achieve. Happy young people will learn and perform better in school than those who are unhappy. They are more energetic, focused and creative and better able to form friendships.

This clear guide shows how to use practical activities to promote thoughtful discussions, engaging, strength-building exercises and confidence boosting fun to enable young people to recognise their personal strengths and use these to build healthy habits, set effective targets and make value-based decisions.